Ariaal Pastoralists of Kenya

CULTURAL SURVIVAL STUDIES
IN ETHNICITY AND CHANGE SERIES

Allyn and Bacon

David Maybury-Lewis and Theodore Macdonald, Jr., Series Editors
Cultural Survival, Inc., Harvard University

Second Edition

Ariaal Pastoralists of Kenya

Studying Pastoralism, Drought, and Development in Africa's Arid Lands

Elliot M. Fratkin
Smith College

Boston • New York • San Francisco
Mexico City • Montreal • Toronto • London • Madrid • Munich • Paris
Hong Kong • Singapore • Tokyo • Cape Town • Sydney

Series Editor: Jennifer Jacobson
Editorial Assistant: Amy Holborow
Marketing Manager: JoAnne Sweeney
Editorial-Production Service: Omegatype Typography, Inc.
Composition and Prepress Buyer: Linda Cox
Cover Administrator: Joel Gendron
Electronic Composition: Omegatype Typography, Inc.

For related titles and support materials, visit our online catalog at
www.ablongman.com.

A previous edition of this volume appeared under the title *Ariaal
Pastoralists of Kenya: Surviving Drought and Development in Africa's
Arid Lands.*

ISBN: 0-205-39142-7

Printed in the United States of America

10 9 8 7 6 5 4 3   08 07 06

To Kawab Bulyar (1942–2002)
Rendille scholar, peacemaker, and friend

Contents

Tables and Figures

Foreword to the Series

Cultural Survival is an organization founded in 1972 to defend the human rights of indigenous peoples, who are those, like the Indians of the Americas, who have been dominated and marginalized by peoples different from themselves. Since the states that claim jurisdiction over indigenous peoples consider them aliens and inferiors, they are among the world's most underprivileged minorities, facing a constant threat of physical extermination and cultural annihilation. This is no small matter, for indigenous peoples make up approximately five percent of the world's population. Most of them wish to become successful ethnic minorities, meaning that they be permitted to maintain their own traditions even though they are out of the mainstream in the countries where they live. Indigenous peoples hope therefore for multi-ethnic states that will tolerate diversity in their midst. In this their cause is the cause of ethnic minorities worldwide and is one of the major issues of our times, for the vast majority of states in the world are multi-ethnic. The question is whether states are to accept and live peaceably with ethnic differences, or whether they will treat them as an endless source of conflict.

Cultural Survival works to promote multi-ethnic solutions to otherwise conflictive situations. It sponsors research, advocacy, and publications which examine situations of ethnic conflict, especially (but not exclusively) as they affect indigenous peoples, and suggests solutions for them. It also provides technical and legal assistance to indigenous peoples and organizations.

This series of monographs entitled "The Cultural Survival Studies in Ethnicity and Change" is published in collaboration with Allyn and Bacon (the Pearson Education Group.) It will focus on problems of ethnicity in the modern world and how they affect the interrelations between indigenous peoples, ethnic groups, and the state.

The studies will focus on the situations of ethnic minorities and of indigenous peoples, who are a special kind of ethnic minority, as they try to defend their rights, their resources and their ways of life within modern states. Some of the volumes in the series will deal with general themes, such as ethnic conflict, indigenous rights, socioeconomic development, or multiculturalism. These volumes will contain brief case studies to illustrate their general arguments. Meanwhile the series as a whole plans to publish a larger number of books that deal in depth with specific cases. It is our conviction that good case studies are essential for a better understanding of issues that arouse such passion in the world today, and this series will provide them. Its emphasis nevertheless will be on relating the particular to the general in the comparative contexts of national or international affairs.

The books in the series will be short, averaging 100 to 150 pages in length, and written in a clear and accessible style aimed at students and the general reader. They are intended to clarify issues that are often obscure or misunderstood and that are not treated succinctly elsewhere. It is our hope, therefore, that they will also prove useful as reference works for scholars, activists, and policy makers.

David Maybury-Lewis
Theodore Macdonald, Jr.
Cultural Survival, Inc.
96 Prospect Street
Cambridge, MA 02139
(617) 441-5400 fax: (617) 441-5417

Preface

The image of the Maasai warrior, resplendent in his red cloth and long braided hair while leaning on his spear, is a familiar one on the tourist brochures of Kenya or Tanzania. Yet the future of Maasai herders and other livestock-keeping pastoralists of East Africa is an uncertain one, threatened by land loss, population pressure, economic marginalization, and political conflicts. As Africa enters the new millennium, its livestock-keeping peoples face greater challenges to their economies and pastoral way of life than any recent time. This book focuses on the social life, cultural ecology, and current situation of Ariaal pastoralists of northern Kenya, showing how these people have survived vicissitudes of drought, population growth, and political conflict as they wrest a living off their animals in the arid region of northern Kenya. This book also demonstrates how some Ariaal are engaging in agriculture or moving to towns to take advantage of new opportunities in employment, marketing livestock and crops, and sending their children to schools. And finally, this books presents a picture of how one anthropologist conducts fieldwork, both in terms of methods used and everyday problems I encountered.

I am delighted that Jennifer Jacobson at Allyn and Bacon asked me to prepare a second edition of Ariaal Pastoralists. This book has been successful in college classrooms, owing, I've been told, to its readable discussion of contemporary problems of East African pastoralists in general, and its portrayal of Ariaal people in particular. This was my intention with the first edition, and I welcome the opportunity to re-engage the ethnography to accomplish several objectives.

The first objective is to bring students up to date on the transition Ariaal and neighboring pastoral groups have been recently undergoing from isolated and self-sufficient livestock pastoralists to more settled groups seeking new economic opportunities as social, economic, and environmental conditions change. Most Ariaal remain committed to livestock production, a sensible choice in an environment generally too dry for agriculture and where the market for livestock, particularly cattle, has been steadily increasing. But Ariaal, like other East African herders, are increasingly settling near towns or taking up agriculture or agro-pastoralism where possible. Some individuals have gone into shop-keeping, livestock trading, or, if educated, have found jobs in government offices or with non-government organizations (NGOs). As Ariaal diversify their livestock herds (keeping a mix of camels, cattle, goats and sheep), so too do they diversify their economic options while still maintaining a broad network of kin, age-mates and friends they can rely on for aid.

A second objective is to engage the student in some of the processes of anthropological fieldwork. To this end, I have expanded what was a short introductory section in the first edition to a new chapter 2, Studying the Ariaal. Here I share not only a few stories of my experiences (always fun for both myself and students in the classroom), but some of the daily work anthropologists do when studying other cultures and writing ethnographic and scientific works. As the focus of my research shifted, so too did my fieldwork methods, from studying Ariaal as a "participant observer" in the 1970s, to conducting economic surveys in the 1980s, to engaging in a large interdisciplinary study on the social, economic, and health consequences of settling of former pastoralists in northern Kenya in the 1990s. This latter research, carried out over ten years, involved extensive collaborations with other cultural anthropologists, biological anthropologists, historians, economists, public health workers, nurses, and physicians, involving the collaboration by eight field assistants and members of five distinct communities of Ariaal and Rendille. (See Acknowledgments). For three years of this project, we interviewed and surveyed 200 Rendille and Ariaal households in five very different communities, interviewing mothers every two months about their own and their children's diets, illnesses, and economic status. We then measured heights, weights, and other nutritional indices. We found that while livestock pastoralism showed distinct advantages in nutrition over town or farm life, the sedentary communities offered advantages including access to health care, schools, jobs, markets, and steady food supply.

A third objective of this second edition is to provide more discussion about my personal fieldwork experiences. Post-modernist anthropologists make an important critique about the subjectivities of the field researcher coloring their presentation of "the other." While I and other anthropologists engaged in more materialist research (i.e. economic, ecological, health, and political topics) maintain that anthropology should be the study of real people facing real problems, field work experiences are also real and important and say as much about the discipline of anthropology as our objective findings.

Finally, to facilitate readability, I have deleted references in the text to scholarly works that address the issues I raise. While subtracting from a scholarly style, deleting references contributes to a more uninterrupted reading, and my principle objective is to use this monograph in the classroom. I do, however, list important works in the References for students pursuing the study of pastoralists in arid lands in more detail.

Pastoralists are struggling to maintain their livestock economy based on mobile herding of cattle, camels, goats and sheep. But many are seeking to diversify their economy by taking up agriculture, agro-pastoralism, or town life. By introducing readers to the lives and experiences of Ariaal pastoralists, I hope to show strengths and weaknesses of current development models, preferring those that focus on appropriate development that does not disrupt social life, degrade the environment, or simply try to end pastoral production in Africa's arid lands. I am delighted and honored that Cultural Survival, an organization long dedicated to promoting the survival and integrity of indigenous peoples, has included this book in their series of topical monographs dealing with social change.

A note on spelling. The Ariaal are bilingual in Rendille (a Cushitic language related to Somali) and Samburu (a dialect of Maa, a Nilotic language), but most Ariaal prefer to speak Samburu, which is the language I used in my fieldwork. Spelling of Ariaal words is based on Mol's (1978) Maasai dictionary, while Rendille spelling follows the writings of Schlee (1989). In keeping with other spellings of Samburu, Samburu masculine prefixes are written as *l-* as in *loiboni, loibonok* (diviners), rather than *ol-oiboni, il-oibonok* as in Maasai, and the feminine prefixes are written as *n*, or as *nkiteng, nkishu* (cow, cattle) instead of *en-kiteng, en-kishu* as in Maasai.

Most of the African words used in the text can be pronounced by following Spanish or Swahili pronunciation of vowel sounds *a, e, i, o,* and *u* and their diphthongs (*ae, ai,* etc.). Speakers of Nilotic languages make an interesting "eng/k'" sound as a glottal stop (almost a click in the back of their throat), as in the words *nkang* (homestead or village, pronounced (eng/k-ahng) or nKai (God, pronounced eng/k-ai).

Acknowledgments

I extend my appreciation to the people among the Ariaal, Rendille, and Samburu who so graciously accepted me into their midst, and who cooperated on so many levels in my research in Marsabit District. In particular I thank my adopted family of Lekati Leaduma and my lifelong friend Lugi Lengesan. I also thank my field assistants Larian Aliyaro, AnnaMarie Aliyaro, and Kawab Bulyar, and Patrick Ngoley in Korr, and Korea Leala and Daniel Lemoille in Karare and Songa villages, and finally Kevin Smith for his friendship and supervision of the 1994–1997 field study. My constant appreciation is extended to my ongoing collaborators Eric Abella Roth (University of Victoria, Canada) and partner-spouse Marty Nathan MD (I hope she finds time to read this edition!). I also thank the various researchers who have collaborated with our research on Rendille sedentarization including biological anthropologists Bettina Shell-Duncan (University of Washington) and Benjamin Campbell (Boston University), health educator Elizabeth Ngugi (University of Nairobi), social anthropologist John Galaty (McGill University), economist John McPeak (Syracuse University), and historian Richard Waller (Bucknell University). I would like to thank the Office of the President, Republic of Kenya for their assistance and permission in carrying out this research, to the many officials in Marsabit District who facilitated my research, and to the faculty and staff at the Institute of African Studies, University of Nairobi, who have long provided an academic home and refuge. Funding for various stages of my research in Kenya was provided by the

National Science Foundation, Smithsonian Institution, National Geographic Society, Social Science Research Council, Mellon Foundation, and Smith College.

I wish to thank Jennifer Jacobson, my editor at Allyn and Bacon, and to Dusty Friedman at the Book Company, for their work on this second edition. I would like to thank the reviewers of this book: Vicki K. Bentley-Condit, Grinnell, College; and Janet MacGaffey, Bucknell University. Finally I wish to extend my appreciation to David Maybury-Lewis, director of Cultural Survival in Cambridge Massachusetts, both for his courageous and long standing work in behalf of indigenous peoples, and for his supervision with Theodore MacDonald of Allyn and Bacon's series *Ethnic Conflict and Social Change*.

Ariaal—Studying An East African Pastoralist Society

Ariaal are a pastoral society of northern Kenya who form a bridge culture between highland cattle-keeping Samburu (Maasai speakers) and lowland Rendille camel pastoralists (Cushitic speakers) distantly related to the Somali. Although often merged with either Samburu or Rendille by outsiders including Kenya census takers, Ariaal see themselves as a distinct group with their own social history. Moreover, where today many Rendille have settled near towns, keeping their livestock in distant camps, Ariaal continue to subsist off and live with their large herds of cattle, camels, and small stock (goats and sheep) in the isolated mountains and deserts of Marsabit District, Kenya's driest region.

Northern Kenya is isolated and undeveloped compared to the rest of the country, where the major populations live in the central highlands, Lake Victoria, and the Indian Ocean Coast. With low rainfall and few rivers, its deserts and mountains are inhabited mainly by nomadic pastoralists, including Turkana, Samburu, Rendille, Boran, Gabra, and Somali. When I first came to Kenya in the 1970s, Marsabit District, the country's largest district, had only 80,000 people out of a total Kenyan population of twenty-two million. The district had only two secondary schools, two hospitals, and no paved roads. Today, there are still no paved roads, and most of the people still herd camels, cattle, goats, and sheep for a living, but there has been substantial change. One-third of the pastoral population now live in towns and farms, mainly near the district capital of Marsabit town on Marsabit Mountain, although most people still have some contact with their pastoralist relatives herding livestock in the desert below. Despite these changes, the district remains isolated and often ignored by the government based in Nairobi.

Between 1974 and 1976, I lived with one large nomadic community of Ariaal, the clan settlement of Lewogoso Lukumai who herded their large herds of camels, cattle, and small stock along the eastern base of the Ndoto Mountains in the western part of Marsabit District. Life was very much determined by seasonal rhythms of brief rains, bringing rich but temporary pasture, followed by long dry periods. In 1976 the rains failed altogether, and I endured the prolonged drought with the Ariaal. But drought is a regular feature of the landscape, "the long hunger" (la'amai lo'odo) which ends only when God (n'gai) chooses to let rain fall again. In the meantime, one moves one's animals in search of pasture and water, which will yield milk, the staple food, to the human population.

I returned to Marsabit in 1985, this time accompanied by my physician wife Marty Nathan and six-year-old daughter, Leah. Where before I had seen another vehicle once every six weeks or so, now we saw or heard trucks, Land Rovers, and small planes almost daily, bringing materials and food to the missionary stations and development projects. These organizations had flooded the region in the 1980s following the Sahelian Famine of the 1970s and the Ethiopian Famine of 1984. Northern Kenya became a locus for famine-relief work of church missions and other nongovernment organizations (NGO's) such as World Vision, as well as the large bilateral German aid and the multilateral United Nations UNESCO project. Nearly one-half of the 25,000 Rendille had settled in small mission towns of Korr, Kargi, and Laisamis, living on grains distributed by the missions, or seeking paid work as herders, watchmen, or government employees. UNESCO's

Integrated Program in Arid Lands (IPAL), had established stations in Ngurunit, Korr, Marsabit, and on Mt. Kulal, and was engaged in promoting livestock marketing to reduce perceived over-grazing of the range land. During the 1990s, I, Marty Nathan, and Eric Roth studied the health and social effects of pastoral sedentarization, looking in particular at how women and children have been affected by changes in diet and livelihoods associated with town life.

Many Rendille pastoralists have settled around the church mission-based towns of Korr and Kargi, although they still continue to raise livestock which must be kept many miles from their settlements due to lack of pasture. Some Rendille and Ariaal have taken up agriculture in the highland communities of Songa and Nasikakwe on Marsabit Mountain. Most Ariaal, however, have continued their pastoral existence raising their animals in the lowlands, or living in sedentary highland communities on Marsabit Mountain where they can keep cattle. While some Ariaal have taken up farming on the mountain, most have resisted sedentarization (settling) and have continued their pastoral life. I believe the Ariaal are able to maintain their pastoral lifestyle because they have a more generalized pastoral strategy, living near mountains with mixed herds of cattle, camels, goats and sheep, while the Rendille depend almost exclusively on large numbers of camels and small stock which must be herded in distant camps due to low rainfall in the Rendille area. Living in close proximity to animals enables the Ariaal access to milk for subsistence and surplus animals to trade and market. Furthermore, the Ariaal have greater access to grazing lands than the Rendille, as they utilize their broad ties of intermarriage, descent, and friendship with both Samburu and Rendille clans and can herd in their areas.

This book describes how the Ariaal survive in the austere and isolated region of northern Kenya. My approach to understanding Ariaal survival combines cultural ecology—how humans as social groups adapt to different kinds of environments—and political economy—how humans' material conditions of life are affected by power differentials and relations within and between social groups. This approach seeks to understand how communities utilize natural resources to support their members while simultaneously dealing with other social groups, who may be larger, hostile, and dominating. As pastoralists, the Ariaal survive in desert terrain by both the raising of domestic livestock for subsistence and trade, and by creating and maintaining ties of alliance with (or alternatively waging war against) neighboring pastoral groups. Although northern Kenya may be physically isolated from the rest of the country, it has not escaped Kenya's rapidly expanding capitalist economy, particularly in terms of providing livestock to larger national markets. Consequently, Ariaal society, like that of Maasai and other pastoralists, is steadily undergoing a transformation from a subsistence to capitalist economy, but entering it at its lowest rungs.

This book is organized as follows: Chapter 1 introduces the concept of pastoralism and describes my fieldwork experiences. Chapter 2 discusses current problems experienced by Kenyan pastoralists including population growth, loss of herding lands to farmers, ranchers, and game parks; problems of drought, famine, and political violence. It compares the situation of the Ariaal to those of Maasai, Turkana, and Rendille pastoralists. Chapter 3 focuses on Ariaal culture and identity, Chapter 4 focuses on their livestock production system, and Chapter 5 describes Ariaal community organization and life in a Lewogoso Lukumai settlement. Chapter 6 discusses recent changes affecting the Ariaal including the growth of towns and farms, and concludes with some suggestions about appropriate development in Africa's arid lands.

THE ARIAAL

The Ariaal are a population of about 10,000 who raise camels, cattle, goats, and sheep in the rugged terrain of mountains and deserts in Marsabit District in northern Kenya. Many Ariaal families descend from the larger Rendille people, a tightly integrated society of about 25,000 who formerly subsisted exclusively off camel, goats, and sheep. But the Ariaal are also closely related to a distinctly different cultural tradition, that of the Samburu, a Maasai people of 100,000 who subsist on cattle and small stock production in the highlands and plains to the west in Samburu District. The Ariaal, Samburu, and Rendille share similar cultural features, including segmentary descent organization (where each community is made up of distinct and autonomous clan families) and the institution of named age-sets where whole sets of men collectively pass through the age grades of child, warrior, and elder. The Ariaal are affiliated with the Samburu clans and age-sets and are considered Samburu by the Rendille, yet because they also speak Rendille and keep camels as well as cattle the Samburu treat them as Rendille. The name 'Ariaal' is used locally to distinguish those mixed groups of Samburu/Rendille who speak Samburu and raise camels as well as cattle.

The area inhabited by the Ariaal is rugged and isolated, made up of both mountain and lowland desert terrain (Figure 1.1). The Ndoto Mountains, which separate Samburu and Marsabit Districts, are tall peaks reaching 2500 meters (8125 feet), and provide the main source of rain for rivers that flow into the deserts below. Ariaal graze their cattle in the highland valleys of these rivers (particularly the Milgis and Merille Rivers), but few settlements are located there except those depending exclusively on cattle and small stock. Most Ariaal live in the flat lowlands below the mountains, where their camels may graze without suffering too many ticks and insects found in the highlands. In addition to the large lowland settlements, about 4000 Ariaal make their home on Marsabit Mountain near the district capital of Marsabit town, located about 150 km northeast of the Ndoto Mountains. Marsabit Mountain has attracted new settlers from Rendille and Ariaal who have taken up agriculture in its watered forests. The mountain is also home to Burji farmers from Ethiopia, and to Boran cattle pastoralists. There has been periodic conflict and competition between Rendille and Boran over water, grazing, and now, farming rights, on the mountain.

Between the Ndoto Mountains and Mt. Marsabit lies the broad and flat Kaisut Desert, which is occupied by Rendille

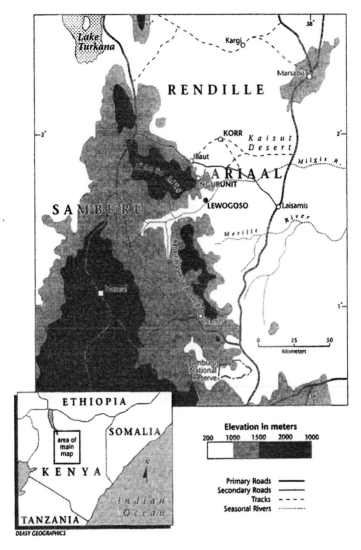

FIGURE 1.1 Location of Ariaal

camel-keeping settlements. The Rendille lived exclusively off their camel and small stock herds until the famines of the 1970s and 1980s forced many to settle in the small towns. To the north of the Rendille is the Chalbi Desert bordering Lake

Turkana and Ethiopia, inhabited by Gabra camel pastoralists, Boran cattle pastoralists, and Dasenech agro-pastoralists on the shores of Lake Turkana. To the west live the Turkana, lifelong enemies of Rendille and Samburu. All of these groups have raided and counter raided each other for livestock, with raids intensifying during the extensive droughts of the 1990s.

Although there have been many changes in the twenty-five years I have worked in this area, I find it remarkable that the majority of Ariaal are living very much as I first found them in the 1970s, subsisting on the milk of their camels and cattle, and trading livestock to buy grains, tea, and sugar at the shops in town. Most Ariaal live with their animals, preferring to live in their large but mobile communities rather than settle in town. Their pastoral economy remains resilient and viable, and livestock continue to be the center of their economy and cultural life.

PASTORALISM—AN ADAPTATION TO ARID LANDS

Pastoralists are people who rely on domestic animals for the majority of their subsistence. They consume milk, meat, blood, and sell animals or their products (wool, leather, cheese) to purchase other foods and necessary commodities. Pastoralists include cattle keepers of East Africa (e.g., Maasai and Samburu), West Africa (Fulani or Peul); camel pastoralists of North Africa and Arabia (Tuareg and Bedouins), sheep pastoralists of the Middle East (Qashq'ai and Baluch of Iran), horse nomads of Mongolia, yak herders of Tibet, reindeer herders of Lapland and Siberia. Pastoralism is distinguished from livestock ranching by the fact that herds are taken to pasture and water, rather than having fodder brought to them, and consequently pastoral populations are mobile (or nomadic), moving herds and herders over wide areas. Pastoralists are considered nomadic when the entire community moves over wide distances (as among Tuareg of Mali or Chukchee of Siberia); others, like the Ariaal and Maasai, are semi-sedentary and herd their animals between seasonal pastures, a system known as transhumance.

Some pastoralists combine dryland farming with livestock keeping, called agro-pastoralism, as practiced by groups such as the Nuer of Sudan and Tswana of Botswana. Increasingly many African pastoralists are taking up some cultivation of grains to supplement their pastoral diets, as among Maasai in Tanzania and Fulani in Niger. The political and social forms pastoral societies take range from autonomous kinship groups (as among Samburu and Maasai) to highly centralized polities (as among Qashq'ai confederation of Iran or the Mongols of the thirteenth century).

A fundamental goal of a herd owner is to maintain enough animals to produce food (milk, meat, or blood) to support the family (or household) group, and to have a sufficiently large labor force (from the household) to provide pasture, water, and security to the herds. East African herders raise more female than male animals to produce milk for both humans and nursing livestock, as well as ensure against periodic loss. Male animals are kept for transport, meat, trade, and to satisfy social obligations such as marriage payments.

Not all people who raise livestock are pastoralists. Ranchers are business people involved in the market economy who raise livestock as a commodity, mainly to provide beef, leather, or wool. While cattle or sheep may range extensively in ranches in the western United States or Australia, their management and herding is done by a small number of people who are paid for their labor. In contrast, pastoralism is a family enterprise, where all members of the household—men and women, young and old—participate in production tasks such as milking animals or spinning wool, and where animals are kept for the household subsistence. Furthermore, while livestock are almost always individually owned by pastoral families, land is seldom privatized but is a shared communal resource, where rights to graze or water are held by local kin groups. A recent phenomenon for pastoralists is the encouragement by international development agencies like the World Bank and USAID to take up private ranching rather than communal herding to improve livestock productivity and commerce. However, as I describe in Chapter 2, privatization of the range and commoditization of pastoralist economies often leads to impoverishment as large numbers of former pastoralists no longer have any place to graze their animals.

A key feature of pastoralist survival in arid lands is the ability to move in order to find pasture and water for their animals. Mobility is based in part on ecological factors, including variation in terrain, rainfall, location of rivers, and variety of vegetation and salt resources. Successful pastoralism also depends on the creation and maintenance of extensive social ties to people spread out over a broad geographical area; ties which are developed through marriage, descent, or personal friendships and cemented by ritual and gifts of livestock.

Unfortunately, traditional pastoral mobility has been restricted by loss of pastoral lands to population pressures (of both humans and livestock), encroachment on important grazing areas by expanding agricultural or other pastoral groups, as well as the creation of commercial ranches and game parks. Because pastoralists are often small minorities and marginal to national economic life, they are often neglected and disempowered by governments made up of people from agricultural societies who have little understanding towards or sympathy for the needs and lives of their pastoralist populations. Furthermore, international donor countries which include the leading developed countries of North America, Europe, and Japan, promote globalization and the integration of the less developed world in the world capitalist economy, promoting privatization and export marketing. For African pastoralists, World Bank and US Agency for International Development policies have led to privatization of formerly communal grazing lands into ranches and the commercialization of the livestock economy. Some of these countries including England and France have had colonial relations with African countries in the past and share prejudices towards pastoralists as primitive, uneducated, and wasteful.

Despite these policies, pastoralism in Africa has proven surprisingly resilient. Raising cattle, camels, goats and sheep has provided a steady supply of food for herding households living in arid regions, and pastoralists have benefited from the increased trade and demand for livestock products. But pastoralism is undergoing a major transition in Africa at this time, as pastoralists seek ways of combining agriculture, urban opportunities, and livestock raising in new ways. This book is a story of how one of these societies, the Ariaal, are undergoing this transition.

FIELDWORK WITH THE ARIAAL

I came to live with the Ariaal quite by accident, although I had long wanted be an anthropologist and live with pastoral nomads in Africa. I had studied anthropology as an undergraduate at the University of Pennsylvania and obtained a Masters degree in anthropology from the London School of Economics. For my Ph.D. work (which I completed at the Catholic University of America), I wanted to study isolated agro-pastoralist groups along the Omo River in southwestern Ethiopia. In 1974, with funds from the University of London and the Smithsonian Institution, I flew to Nairobi intending to reach Lake Turkana and the Omo River from the Kenya side. Driving an old BSA 250 cc motorcycle, I headed north around Mt. Kenya through the deserts of Marsabit District toward Ethiopia. When I reached the small town of Marsabit, however, I learned there had been a *coup d'etat* against Haile Selassie in Ethiopia and that the border was now closed. The new military government (soon to be led by the bloody regime of Haile Miriam Mengestu) had no interest in foreigners like myself conducting research in the countryside.

I sat in a dusty bar in Marsabit town wondering what to do. Marsabit town lies on top of a broad volcanic mountain 1500 meters high; and although situated smack in the center of a hot lowland desert, it is covered in dense tropical forest. This mountain is home to some of Kenya's largest elephants, protected in a forest reserve. While drinking my tea and eating chapati bread, a boy about fourteen years old asked if I would like to see the elephants in the reserve. When I told him "not today," he thought a minute and asked, "Would you like to come to my village and see traditional African dances?" This was more to my anthropological liking, and I readily agreed.

We drove on my motorcycle seventeen kilometers south of Marsabit town on the main road, confronted once by an elephant on a bridge (my fearless guide yelling "Speed up, he has to back up before he can charge us!"). Miraculously we arrived in his village of Karare, a large Ariaal community consisting of four large circles of houses surrounding cattle enclosures. I could see there was indeed dancing going on, but this was not a performance for tourists. At the far end of the largest settlement, scores of warriors were dancing in a tight circle, twirling their spears and snapping their long braided hair as they moved forward into a waiting group of adolescent girls, singing in soprano a response to the warriors' deep chorus. The dancers wore grim and serious expressions, and I stayed at a distance with the older folks and small children, thrilled with the spectacle.

Off to one side stood a short man dressed in a green cloth (unlike the other men wearing white or red clothes), who wore a serious and intimidating expression. As the warriors moved past him in the circle, he marked their foreheads and shoulders with a yellow powder. The small man in green was a *laibon* medicine man, and he was protecting the warriors with ritual medicine or *ntasim* (pronounced en-*tah*-sim). His name was Lekati Leaduma, and we were soon to become lifelong friends.

I had arrived in the middle of an important ritual, one of the large *mugit* ox-slaughters that Samburu and Ariaal warriors hold during their fourteen-year period as *murrani* (warriors). This particular ritual, the Mugit of the Name (*mugit lenkarna*), was being repeated for all members of the Lorokushu clan (of whom most of Karare's residents belonged) to remedy an unfortunate event. It seems that the age-set leader (the *launon*) for Lorokushu clan, a man chosen for his leadership and skills of negotiation, had been killed trying to break up a fight between two Ariaal warriors. His death was very unpropitious for the clan as a whole, and all Lorokushu warriors had to repeat the *mugit* and replace the dead *launon*.

I was offered a house to stay in that night, a small oval dome of sisal mats and leather skins tied over a wooden frame. Inside, the house was divided with the cooking hearth and visitor's area near the door, and a sleeping area lined by cow skins in the back half. The house was old, its sisal roof mats black and shiny from the fireplace smoke. I was enthralled by the experience, listening to the quiet voices and ruminating cattle outside, looking at the beaded milk containers and leather storage bags tied to the wall frame, peacefully drifting asleep. Suddenly, I woke up as I felt small stings on my legs and back. They were flea bites, and they were everywhere—on my legs, in my hair, under my arms. And there was nothing I could do about it. I pulled a sheet over my head and fell into a fitful sleep, my fantasies of living in a Rousseauian paradise slipping into nightmares about snakes, scorpions, and spiders.

The next morning I was awakened by the "Samburu alarm clock"—flies buzzing around my head and landing on my face, nose, and ears. I got up quickly and walked outside. It was very misty, one could hardly see to the next house. But I could hear metal cow bells ringing and the sound of women's voices gently singing to their cattle as they milked them. Outside one house, two warriors were leaning casually on their long spears. Ariaal warriors, like Rendille, Samburu, and Maasai, are striking to look at. They wear their hair in long woven braids dyed red with red ochre and fat, cover their bodies with red cloths slung casually over their shoulders or worn around their waists, and carry a myriad of weapons including slender spears, a long sword sheathed in leather, and the ever present *rungu*, a wooden club with a large metal gear on the end. For fourteen years, from the time of their initiation by public circumcision until they marry and become elders, warriors lead a distinctive and separate life. They live apart from the main settlements, never eating food in the presence of a woman (except to take milk in their mother's house), and spend most of their time living with fellow warriors in livestock camps, or among the more sedentary Maasai, in their own permanent warrior villages.

The warriors greeted me, *Sopa murr'ata!* ("Greetings, age-mate"). One of them flicked his head and asked me if I wanted to accompany them to water their cattle at the wells in the forest. I was ready to go; I had my walking boots and baggy military pants, my shoulder bag with notebook, pen, and camera. "Ma'apetin"—"Let's go!"

We left the village and headed toward the large woods of the Marsabit Forest Reserve. Jogging at first, I petered out after a mile. The warriors could easily have run five miles, but slowed down to wait for me. Soon our path became a winding trail through the mountain woods of tall hardwoods, fig trees, and vines. After some miles we came to l-chota, a series of wells with hundreds of cattle and scores of warriors about. Several warriors stopped to shake my hand, while others glared at me with unfriendly faces that told me this was not a good time to take pictures. My companions motioned me to one of the wells, and soon had me working, passing water buckets up from the well in a three-man chain. I enjoyed the rhythm of the work, adding my voice to their singing, to all our delight.

When we finished watering the cattle, my companion flicked a finger on the side of his neck and motioned me to follow him and his two friends. The flick at the neck, I soon realized, meant lunch time, specifically blood tapped from a living animal. We approached a large gray ox (castrated male), and as one warrior held it by the horns, the other tied a long leather cord tightly about the neck, exposing a large jugular vein pulsating on the side of a neck. With a small bow, a short arrow was shot into the vein, popping out immediately as a steady flow of blood poured into a woven bowl. After a liter or so of blood was collected, the warrior released the leather cord and the blood continued its flow back in the animal, hardly bleeding at all now. My companion took a swig from the bowl, and smiling in delight, passed it to me. Deciding this would not kill me (I was in strong denial of germ theory at the time), I slowly sipped the frothy blood, surprised at its warmth and salty sweet taste. I had little time to savor the moment. Running quickly into the bushes, I knew I could expect a bout of diarrhea every time I drank blood. I stayed with these warriors about two weeks in their mountain camp, drinking milk and blood, herding and watering cattle during the day, then staying up late at night trying to sing their melancholy but beautiful songs, and join their dances when they visited their girlfriends' villages. It was here that I learned both humility and humor were the two attributes that led the warriors to trust and accept me. Although generally incompetent in most tasks normally performed by warriors (such as milking cattle, killing snakes, or throwing spears and clubs with any accuracy), I always tried to join in. However, sometimes my clumsy enthusiasm was too much for even the most patient of my friends, and I would politely be removed from the dances when the spear I was twirling flew out of my hands, or landed on the foot of the warrior behind me as we jump danced. But the warriors would patiently explain Samburu phrases in pantomime, insisting that I write the words down in my "kivu" (book).

Still, the living conditions were difficult. One evening, as I was scratching at my toes for some time, a warrior removed a large safety pin he wore on his neck beads, and taking my foot in his hand, slowing poked a hole under my toe nail. Quite dramatically, a large white larva emerged, totally grossing me out. I later learned sand fleas laid their eggs in cattle manure and then enter innocent flesh like mine to carry on their life cycle. I decided to wear hard shoes on a permanent basis.

Despite, or perhaps because of, these experiences, I decided I wanted to live and study with these people. I had heard horror stories about other anthropology students, sent by their professors to study some group of people they did not like, and they were not liked in return. Despite the problems in sanitation, I genuinely liked these people, and they liked me. I decided to change my research focus, and after some lengthy negotiations in Nairobi, was able to obtain research permission to conduct anthropological fieldwork in Marsabit District and through the good fortune of a grant from Smithsonian Institution, able to purchase a used short-wheel-base Land Rover in exchange for my *piki-piki* motorcycle.

It took three months to obtain government permission, after which I returned directly to Karare village. As fortune would have it, I was asked by the *laibon* Lekati Leaduma to accompany him to the lowland village of Lewogoso with his friend Lugi Lengesen. I readily agreed, as I preferred to get farther away from Marsabit town and further into the desert. It took us many hours of driving over open terrain and increasingly thick scrub bush, with Lugi walking half the time trying to direct me over a path normally used by cattle and camels.

Finally at dusk we reached Lugi's clan settlement of Lewogoso Lukumai, a large village of over 50 houses, surrounding thorn bush enclosures of animals. As I would measure later, there were 250 people and 600 camels, 500 cattle, and 2000 goats and sheep. About twelve kilometers behind it lay the cloud-covered peaks of the Ndoto Mountains. This was one of the loveliest places I have ever seen. Moreover, Lewogoso was a camel-keeping rather than a highland cattle-keeping village, meaning there was little wet manure and no fleas.

When I first arrived, people treated me politely, but few understood why I was there. I was the first white person anyone in this village had ever seen, except for Lugi who had been to prison during colonial times, when he was a young warrior and was caught raiding cattle. When it became clear to Lewogoso's residents that I was not there to harm anyone, people generally left me alone, viewing me simply as Lugi's guest. Soon after arriving, I began introducing myself to everyone I bumped into outside their houses, trying to chat in the early evenings when the animals were returning and women were milking their animals. After a few weeks, I knew most people by name and had a sense of how people were related to one another. Nearly every married male was a member of the Lewogoso (the "long necks") subclan of Lukumai clan, one of eight large patrilineal sections that made up the Samburu and the Ariaal. This society had no chiefs, except individuals appointed by the government's District Officer. But this individual, although a respected elder, had no authority to make any person do something he did not want to. Rather, elders decided matters collectively, either informally while sitting and playing the *mbau* board game, or more formally when assembled for meetings inside the village.

The oldest man in the village was Leriare, a man who looked as ancient as anyone I have ever seen. He was a member of the Merisho age set (initiated in 1910) and was probably in his late seventies when I first met him. Leriare had outlived his three wives and slept alone in a small house next to the house of his oldest son's first wife. Leriare always had a grumpy scowl on his face, but he was an active and alert old man tending his own goats or carrying firewood to his small house. He never spoke to me much, but one time, he came up to me and demanded, *"Ero!* ("Youth!"), Why don't you give me your hat. It's hot on my head." Much to his surprise, I immediately complied. "Here old man, you use this, I'll find another." That night, Leriare came to the door of my house. Refusing to come in, he thrust a large wooden gourd of milk through the door and said, "Here, this is for you. I don't ever want to hear that you went hungry in this village!" And from then on, Leriare, or one of his grandchildren, brought me a gourd of milk every day I was in the settlement. Visiting Lewogoso in 1996 with my college aged daughter Leah, long after old Leriare had passed away, his oldest son Irionai, now old and wiry as his father, brought me the customary gourd of milk. And although I have given as well as received, my family and I have never gone hungry in Lewogoso village. Reciprocity—gift-giving—is a cornerstone of Ariaal life, and despite the frequent barrage of requests for sugar, tobacco, or flashlights that I was normally subjected to, my friends in Lewogoso have always reciprocated. I feel that I truly belong to Lewogoso clan.

I remained in Lewogoso for eighteen months, leaving every three months or so to spend 3–4 weeks working on my notes at the Institute of African Studies in Nairobi where I had a research affiliation. I also admit that it was great to have a shower, eat an Indian meal, and see a movie while eating a Cadbury Whole Nut chocolate bar. But in short time Nairobi overwhelmed me, and I needed to go back north to Lewogoso. At first I lived in a tent between Lugi's and Leaduma's houses, but after a few weeks, Lugi's eldest wife

Padamu (one of two and later four wives) organized the women to make me a house, a round structure in Rendille fashion but equipped with a small bookshelf, desk and chair.

Although I initially used interpreters (including Kilecho Lendiyo, a nephew of Leaduma's), in time I learned to speak Samburu, although I never gained a vocabulary or grammar superior to a six year old. In fact it was Lugi's six-year-old son, Pantan, who was my first teacher, quizzing me every night on facial nouns (the eyes, the ear, the nose). But it was the warriors who took a strong interest in my language

Old Leriare with My Hat

training, teaching me verb tenses, idioms, and slang, making sure I wrote it all down in my notebook so I could study each night. And finally there was my good friend Lugi, who to this day, speaks fluent "ki-Elliot" and understands most of what I ask or try to say. The trick to good fieldwork is not to worry about how foolish you appear, but get up each time you fall, learn from your mistakes, and laugh along when everyone else is laughing at you. Soon they will be laughing with you.

At first, my research interests focused on studying Ariaal rituals, and particularly the "rites of affliction" practiced by the *laibon* in divining and combating sorcery. I traveled with Leaduma to distant manyattas whenever possible where the Laibon was asked to throw the divination stones and treat people with his ritual medicines. When I successfully brought Leaduma's wife and young son from Samburu District to join him in Lugi's village after a long separation, I was adopted as Leaduma's son and brother to Kanikis, his young boy. That night, after a long celebration feasting on a goat and making long predictions for the entire village, Leaduma exclaimed, "Let no person say there goes the 'white' Leaduma. There are no 'white' Leadumas, there are no 'black' Leadumas, there are only Leadumas!" In addition to studying ritual medicine of the *laibons*, I also studied Samburu herbal medicine with a traditional herbalist named Lemeriwas and an elderly midwife named Lenguye who specialized in women's health.

My first year living at Lewogoso was a period of intense drought (1975), and I became increasingly interested in survival and questions of ecological adaptation to arid lands. It is not unusual to change or modify research topics in the field, but this was a completely new area of interest for me and I had to learn about ecology on my own. I sought out researchers and professionals active in veterinary, plant, and water sciences, some of whom worked with the UNESCO Integrated Project in Arid Lands. I traveled to different communities, livestock camps, and grazing areas, interviewing elders and warriors about cattle, camels, and small stock production. Some of this work was carried out by surveys. I developed a survey form that listed houses by identification

Elliot Fratkin and Ariaal Warrior in Lewogoso Settlement

number, the names and ages of the adults, the names and ages of their children, the amount of bridewealth paid by the groom for the marriage, and the number of lactating animals of all species—cattle, camels, goats, sheep, and donkeys. I chose to ask number of milking animals because I could roughly calculate the total number of animals in each household herd. It was both rude to ask the total number of animals anyone owned, and people would not give you very reliable answers. ("How many cattle do you own?", I would ask, "*Mingi*—Many," was always the reply.) By knowing the number of nursing animals (animals were milked only when they had nursing offspring), I could roughly calculate the total number of animals of every herd each household owned. (For example, I knew from veterinary studies that 66% of Samburu cattle herd are female, of which 50% are lactating at any given time, based on their year-round mating period, 9 months gestation, 8 months lactation period, and 17 month birth interval. A household with 6 nursing calves would then have approximately 12 adult females plus 4 female calves which are 2/3 the total herd, or 24 cattle.) In a similar way I could calculate the herd size of camels, goats, and sheep.

I also developed methods for measuring labor inputs based on time allocation survey techniques used in other anthropological (and industrial) studies. Here, I made unannounced visits to houses chosen at random at different times of the day, recording the age and sex of each person I observed and writing down their activity (e.g., cooking, manufacturing, resting, etc.). Later I coded this data into a 4000 observation data set, of which I could generate age and gender specific tasks. I found, for example, that where adult men spent 33% of their daylight hours in livestock tasks, women spent 14% of their day with animals, mainly in milking. Both adolescent boys and girls spent time with livestock; with boys giving 71% of their time to these tasks and girls 44%. I also determined that household wealth, measured by number of livestock owned, was correlated with the number of household members one had available for herding and livestock tasks. My Ph.D. dissertation ultimately focused on the organization of labor and production in this pastoral society, utilizing in no small part the data generated by these time-allocation studies.

After a few months or so I was treated as a member of the Lewogoso community, but as a rather wealthy member from whom most families could expect gifts of sugar, tea, and a flashlight or cooking pot. Although I was a now part of the Lewogoso community of Ariaal, my status was ambiguous. When I first came, I was unmarried and considered a member of the warrior age-set, but unlike a warrior who lives with his age-mates "in the bush," I had a house in the settlement like a married elder but had no wife. People were tolerant of this identity crisis, and laughed good-naturedly when, asked if I was an elder (*l-paiyen*) or a warrior (*l-murrani*), I replied, "When the elders eat meat in the settlement, I am an elder; when the warriors eat meat in the bush, I am a warrior."

In time, I cultivated friendships with several people, men and women, married and single, who became my "key informants." While anthropologists joke that a key informant is anyone who will talk to you, in fact these individuals were my very prized translators of Ariaal culture,

Letuan an expert on kinship relations, Lenguye the midwife and woman's doctor who led me into the world of herbal medicines, Lemeriwas the herbalist, Leaduma the Laibon diviner, and Lugi Lengesen who knew all the politics and social problems of the Ariaal and Rendille communities. These were friends who looked after me and cared for me as much as I did them. Once I woke up with high fever and excruciatingly painful headache. It was malaria, and all I could do was crawl over to Lugi's wife Padamu's house. For the next week as I came in and out of consciousness, she would be there with a hot cup of tea and persuade me to take the chloroquine I brought necessary to combat this deadly blood parasite.

Lewogoso's warriors treated me as one of their own. I often joined them on herding trips to the mountains, sleeping in the open on a cow skin, subsisting on milk and blood. I carried a spear, sword, and *rungu*, and wore a cloth and beads most of the time (although I kept on good walking shoes rather than wear their "tire" sandals, and I also wore a hat and carried a knapsack with camera, tape recorder, and the necessary toilet paper). I attended moonlit dances with scores of warriors and young women, although it took me some time to learn to twirl my spear without stabbing the warrior behind me. Once a warrior begged me to give him the new spear I had made by a local blacksmith. I declined, as it was a beautiful spear. The exasperated warrior said "You don't even know how to use it!" I replied, "But I need it for the dances!"

By 1976, I had spent one and a half years with Lewogoso community. I had been given several dozen goats and two cows, I had interviewed people about ritual life, plant medicines, and traditional knowledge of livestock production, and I had enjoyed the seclusion and isolation far from my own country. I had enough material for my dissertation, and moreover, I was exhausted (I didn't know until I returned to the United States that I had hepatitis, a very depressing disease). But I was reluctant to leave Africa and I came home slowly, selling my Land Rover and taking trucks, barges, and trains through Sudan and Egypt until I reached Cairo and took a flight home.

I returned in 1985 accompanied by my wife Marty Nathan and six-year-old daughter, Leah. Other anthropologists have remarked on the advantages (and disadvantages) of having one's family along, and these applied to us. My status as a married elder was now secure, allowing me access to the men's shade tree for extensive conversations about livestock and the complexities of Ariaal life. Moreover, the experiences and interactions of Marty and Leah gave me insights into the society that I did not have before. Marty, as a physician working in mission clinics, earned her own reputation as a friend and healer among Ariaal.

A seasoned fieldworker, I was now able to obtain information in a week that previously had taken months to figure out, as I knew what I was looking for and I had prepared questionnaires and interview designs. I never got sick as I had before (with malaria, pneumonia, hepatitis), as Marty kept me on the straight and narrow taking malaria pills and not drinking or eating everything that was offered to me. However, we were scared to death when Leah woke one day convulsing with a serious fever and had to be flown out of Nairobi by the Flying Doctors organization. She recovered quickly, and we never knew what hit her. Today, I make sure that students traveling to African countries have the most up to date guidelines on current health risks and their prevention, which can be obtained from the Centers for Disease Control and Prevention in Atlanta, Ga.

In the 1990s, Marty, anthropologist Eric Roth, and I developed an extensive research project on health and nutrition of women and children, where we and our Ariaal and Rendille assistants interviewed over 200 women and their children in five separate locations (including pastoral Lewogoso, famine relief towns, and sedentarized agricultural communities). We conducted interviews and surveys every two months over a three year period (1994–1997), studying the effects of pastoral sedentarization on the health and economic well being of the different communities. We found that the traditional pastoral diet (made up largely of camel's milk) provides better nutrition to children than town based diets consisting mainly of *posho* (maize meal), and that despite better health interventions in towns, nomadic children were three times less likely to be seriously malnourished than the children living in towns. I discuss this research in more detail in Chapter 6.

I continue to revisit Lewogoso and to see my friends of twenty-five years. Sadly, Lekati Leaduma passed away in 1987, but I have remained close to his son (my brother Kanikis), who is becoming the new *laibon* of the Ariaal. In 1995, I provided a wedding ox so Kanikis could marry, something that gave me great satisfaction. Lugi Lengesen has remained my closest friend, and now over 70 years old, is thinking of settling down on a farm on Marsabit Mountain. Although I helped him build a house in which his third wife lives and raises maize, Lugi still prefers to be with his animals and remains in Lewogoso. I have never regretted my decision to live with and study the Ariaal. I have built a lifetime of friendships and experiences in Africa, which have made cultural anthropology very rewarding to me on a deep and personal level.

The Ariaal represent a pastoral society that, at least for now, has been able to survive in arid lands through their pastoral livestock production system. Theirs is a telling story because it demonstrates that humans are capable of surviving in a variety of physical environments, and within a complex social and political world. Their future is not secure, however, because of further encroachments on their herding environment, competition with growing and rival pastoral populations, and an ever-expanding capitalist economy that seeks to privatize land, livestock, and labor, even in the margins of Africa's arid lands.

2

Drought, Development, and Kenya's Pastoralists

Although livestock-keeping pastoralists occupy over 70% of Kenya's land (580,367 km²), they make up less than one million of Kenya's thirty million people who are mainly peasant farmers or rural and urban wage-workers. Kenya's agricultural groups include Bantu speaking Kikuyu of the central highlands; Kamba, Luyia, and Swahili speakers of the coast; and Nilotic speaking Luo of Lake Victoria. Livestock keeping pastoralists, who occupy Kenya's arid plains and savannas, fall into two large language groups, Nilotes (in the Sudanic family of languages) and Cushites (in the Afro-Asiatic family, which includes Arabic, Amharic, and Hebrew). Nilotic-speaking pastoralists include the Maa-speaking Maasai, Samburu, LChamus, and Ariaal; the Turkana (who are related to Jie and Karimojong of Uganda); and Nandi-speaking agro-pastoralists, including Kalenjin, Kipsigis, and Pokot. Cushitic speakers are populations found in Kenya's northeastern regions bordering Ethiopia and Somalia, and include Rendille, Boran, Gabra, Dasenetch, and Somali (see Figure 2.1).

Pastoralist history in Kenya divides into three periods: pre-colonial, the colonial era (1895–1963), and the post-colonial period since 1963. The nineteenth century was characterized by increasing trade for slaves and ivory from the coast into the interior, pastoral groups such as the Maasai

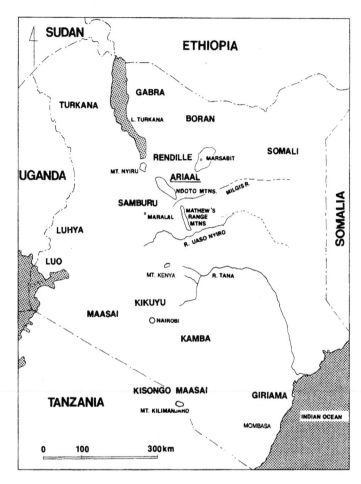

FIGURE 2.1 Peoples of Kenya

dominated the plains and extracted tribute. However, expanding pastoral populations increasingly fought each other for grazing lands. Turkana from Sudan pushed south onto Samburu and Rendille lands, Boran from southern Ethiopia expanded into northern Kenya and competed with Rendille, Samburu, and Somali pastoralists. In southern Kenya, competing Maasai groups fought each other for rich savanna grasslands in the Rift Valley, culminating in the devastating Purko/Laikipiak Maasai wars of the 1870s. By the end of the nineteenth century, East African pastoralists faced severe famine and hardship caused by the hammering combination of drought and the spread of two devastating diseases—smallpox, which ravaged humans, and rinderpest, which decimated their cattle. These diseases were introduced by increasing contact with Europeans and Arab peoples, who had been trading and raiding East Africa for slaves, ivory, and gold since the 1850s. By 1900 Great Britain began to colonize Kenya and Uganda and began construction of a railroad from Mombassa (Kenya) to Kampala (Uganda), directly bisecting Maasai lands.

As Kenya's farmers and pastoralists began to recover from these disasters, European colonial powers were gaining territorial possessions in Africa. The British initially had little interest in Kenya, except as a route for their railroad from Mombassa to the kingdom of BuGanda on Lake Victoria. In short time, however, Britain encouraged the settling of Europeans in the highland areas along Kenya's Rift Valley (what became known as the White Highlands). With African labor coerced from newly formed Native Reserves, the settlers grew coffee, tea, sisal, and tobacco for export, and produced beef and cereals to feed the growing African and (imported) Indian labor force. The Kenya colony grew from 100 European settlers in 1903 to 1000 (owning 4.5 million acres) in 1915 to 4000 (owning 7.5 million acres) in 1953.

The Maasai lost over one-half of their grazing lands, including the rich savannas around Lakes Nakuru and Naivasha, when government treaties in 1904 and 1911 moved them south of the railway line into present day Kajiado and Narok Districts. To the north, Samburu pastoralists gave up the Laikipiak plains to European cattle ranchers in 1934 in exchange for use of the Leroki Plateau in present day Samburu District. Africans were prohibited from growing either crops or livestock for export markets, and the overcrowded and impoverished conditions in the reserves, particularly among disenfranchised Kikuyu farmers, led to wide scale discontent culminating in the Mau Mau rebellion in the 1950s and ultimately independence in 1963.

Following independence, Kenya was pulled directly into the global capitalist economy. International development agencies such as the World Bank and United States Agency for International Development (USAID) encouraged the continued production of export crops (coffee, tea, and cotton, aided by dams and irrigation schemes) as well as industrial development in manufacture of cars, fertilizers, and chemicals. The 1970s was a period of increasing drought and famine, particularly in the pastoral regions, leading to programs of massive famine relief in the north, the development of private ranches in the Maasai regions, and increasing migration of poor pastoralists to towns and cities.

Today Kenya's pastoralists face a variety of problems not directly experienced in their past which threaten their ability to continue raising and living off their livestock herds. These problems are:

DROUGHT AND FAMINE

Periodic drought is a normal feature of East African climate, and pastoralists more than other populations have historically adapted to conditions of low and erratic rainfall and patchy grazing resources through movement of their animals to distant pastures. However, drought and famine in Africa increased dramatically in the second half of the twentieth century, particularly in the Sahelian countries (Senegal, Mauritania, Mali, Niger, Nigeria, Chad, and Sudan) from 1968–1973, and in the East and the Horn of Africa (Ethiopia, Eritrea, Somalia, Djibouti, and northern Kenya) in 1982–1984, 1990–1992, 1996 and 2000. While droughts may be triggered by larger climatic events including global warming and volcanic eruptions, recent African famines (where hundreds of thousands of people have starved to death) are due more directly to civil war and political dislocation, as in Ethiopia, Sudan, and Somalia in the 1980s and 1990s. During these periods, herders lost up to 80% of their small stock and half of their cattle, both to starvation and to infectious diseases that infect the weakened herds, particularly after rains resume.

POPULATION GROWTH

Kenya has one of the world's highest population growth rates (3.0% annual increase), attributed to high but declining total fertility rates (4.7 in Kenya in 2002) coupled with declines in child mortality. However, HIV/AIDS is spreading rapidly, resulting in high mortality among young adults and declining life expectancies (48.7 years for males and 49.9 for females). High population growth has affected urban and rural populations, agricultural as well as pastoral, who increasingly move onto less productive lands to raise their families. When farmers move into the plains for land, pastoralists such as the Maasai find themselves losing herding lands and scarce water resources. In the more arid north where agriculture is possible only in isolated highlands, population growth has led to increasing competition with pastoral neighbors for pasture and water, leading to armed fighting between Turkana and Pokot, Boran and Rendille, Turkana and Samburu, and Somali and Boran herders.

LOSS OF COMMON PROPERTY RESOURCES

Where livestock among most East African pastoralists constitutes individual or family property, access to land (for pasture, water, minerals, and security) is usually held in common as a communal resource (i.e., shared by territorial or kinship groups) or common property open to all. Ignoring traditional land tenure in favor of individual tenure rights, the Kenyan government has encouraged the privatization of communal lands, following policies initiated by the colonial government and encouraged by international donor organizations, including the World Bank and the U.S. Agency for International Development. Following the establishment of "group ranches" in Maasailand in the 1960s, the Kenya government is now promoting private and individual titles, leading to a scramble for land similar to the west in the U.S. in the nineteenth century. In addition, tourism is now Kenya's largest earner of foreign revenue, and pastoralists such as the Maasai are losing herding rights to national game parks including Amboseli, Mara Masai, Tsavo, and Samburu Parks.

COMMODITIZATION, SEDENTARIZATION, AND URBAN MIGRATION

Pastoralists have increasingly shifted economy from subsistence production (producing mainly milk for the household consumption) to commercial production (beef and dairy products for sale both to domestic and export markets). This increased commoditization of the livestock economy has led to major transformations of pastoral society, including increased polarization of pastoralists into "haves" owning private ranches and "have nots," with poor pastoralists working for wealthier kinsmen or migrating to towns in search of low-paying jobs such as watchmen, or, for women, as maids or prostitutes. Moreover, the transition to commoditization and sedentarization has led to shifts in nutrition from protein-rich milk to protein-poor grains, as our recent research shows.

POLITICAL TURMOIL AND CIVIL WAR

Kenya has not avoided ethnic conflict that has plagued Africa and much of the world, although they have not reached the level experienced in Rwanda, Sudan, and Somalia. Pastoralists have suffered in countries where they constitute ethnic minorities discriminated against by more powerful agricultural states. In Kenya's north, inter-pastoralist stock-raiding is increasingly violent as automatic weapons make their way into pastoralist hands from neighboring Ethiopia, Somalia, Sudan, and Uganda.

A comparison of the Ariaal's situation to that of three other Kenyan pastoralist groups—the Maasai, Turkana, and

Rendille—illustrates the current problems pastoral populations share.

THE MAASAI: LOSS OF LANDS

Few other African societies have been as romanticized and popularized by Europeans and Americans, while simultaneously neglected and underdeveloped, as the Maasai. Despite their image as "free and noble warriors," the Maasai have seen their grazing lands continuously reduced by colonial appropriation, the creation of national game parks, the steady incursions of agriculturalists, and most recently by the creation of private titles to individual ranches which are dividing the remaining land.

The Maasai are a population of over 350,000 residing in Kenya and Tanzania; their language is shared by another 300,000 people, including the Samburu, LChamus, and Ariaal in Kenya and the Arusha and Il-Parakuyo in Tanzania. Never a single political entity, the Maasai are composed of a dozen independent groups, including the Kisongo of Tanzania, and Purko, Loita, Matapato, Kaputei, Sikiari, Loitokitok, Damat, Keekonyukie, ilKankeri, and Lo'odokilani Maasai of Kenya.

In the nineteenth century Maasailand stretched in an hour-glass shape from present day Marsabit and Laikipia Districts in Northern Kenya down the broad plains of the Rift Valley lakes (Baringo, Naivasha, Nakuru) to the savanna grasslands of the Maasai Steppe of northern Tanzania, encompassing present-day Serengeti Park. Colonial intrusion cut Maasai land in half, first as an international boundary between British Kenya and German Tanganiyka in 1885, and again in 1911 when the British pushed the Kenyan Maasai south of the Mombassa–Uganda railroad (which passes through Nairobi) on to a single reserve in southern Kenya, later administered as Kajiado and Narok Districts. European settlers took the most important Maasai dry-season water and grazing lands for their farms and ranches, including the Ngong Hills and Lakes Naivasha and Nakuru; the Mau escarpment in Kenya; and the highland reserves of Mts. Kilimanjaro and Meru in Tanganiyka (a British colony following Germany's defeat in World War I).

Confined to 35,000 km^2 in Kenya and 60,000 km^2 in Tanzania (60% of their pre-colonial range), the Maasai were further restricted from grazing their cattle in the large game reserves, including the vast Serengeti Park and Ngorongoro Crater in Tanzania, and, in Kenya, the Nairobi National Park, Amboseli, Tsavo, Mara Masai, and Samburu Game Parks. Government prohibitions arose from concern that the pastoralist herds were responsible for degradation to savanna lands, threatening the wildlife of giraffe, wildebeest, and elephants important to tourism revenues and settler recreation, despite ecological evidence to the contrary.

The Maasai also faced competition for land by both expanding agriculturalists and commercial enterprises creating grain and dairy estates, particularly following independence in Kenya in 1963. Kajiado District's population grew from 22,000 in 1948 to 86,000 in 1969, to 149,000 in 1979, to 250,000 in 1989, and to 350,000 in 1999, reflecting an average growth of 3.5% annually. While some of this population growth reflects improved health care and rising reproductive rates among Maasai, most of the growth reflects migration by Kikuyu and Kamba agriculturalists onto Maasai lands to escape the overcrowding of the central highlands.

Not all immigrant farmers into Maasailand have been poor, however. Since independence, there have been substantial increases in large-scale commercial enterprises taking over Maasai lands. In Narok District, 320,000 hectares of land have been sold to land speculators and farmers since 1980, where the rich and arable land of the Mau Escarpment is now producing commercial wheat and barley. Much of this land has been leased, rented, or sold outright by Maasai owners, who can no longer graze their animals on their former lands.

The ability of Maasai to transfer land individually is a recent phenomenon brought about when the Kenyan government encouraged citizens to title their own land in the 1960s. In traditional Maasai society, no Maasai "owned" grazing or water resources, rather land was shared by all members of the *olosho* (territorial section). Following independence, the Kenyan government began to allocate individual sections of land (usually that with the best pasture and permanent water) to influential members of the community. It was believed that individual ranches would better contribute to the national livestock market than communal pastoralism, and would set an example for other Maasai. But few Maasai benefited from the early privatization, nor did they keep their animals from grazing on the private ranches. In 1968, with support from USAID and the World Bank, Kenya proposed "group ranches," which conferred formal and legal land tenure to a community of co-residents. The Maasai in general accepted the group ranch concept as a way to prevent continuing agricultural encroachment on their land and to acquire legal tenure enabling them to qualify for loans and the development of wells and veterinary cattle dips (to kill ticks).

In the 1980s, with encouragement from the United States and the World Bank and its structural adjustment programs encouraging privatization, Kenya titled much of the common land in the semi-arid regions to individual owners, usually in five to ten hectare plots for small holders growing maize and other market crops (one hectare is 100 × 100 meters or 2.47 acres). There has been a virtual stampede for land claims, especially in the Maasai areas of Kajiado and Narok Districts, as farmers as well as Maasai themselves rush to claim title to some land, lest they lose it all. The process of privatizing land to individual hands has led to permanent loss of common grazing lands through sales to non-Maasai and commercial ventures.

In addition to losing land to ranchers and farmers, Maasai have seen grazing lands lost to national game parks. Tourist revenues now make up 45% of Kenya's GDP (gross domestic product), and international conservation groups have urged the Kenyan and Tanzanian government to reduce the amount of cattle previously permitted to graze in certain parks. In 1959 in Tanzania (then British ruled Tanganyika), Maasai agreed to abandon the rich plains of the Serengeti National Park (14,760 km²) in exchange for grazing privileges on the external slopes of the Ngorongoro Conservation Area (8,292 km²), but were prohibited from practicing any cultivation in the area. Today, the Maasai pastoral economy is on the verge of collapse in the Ngorongoro area. Furthermore, the nutritional status of local Maasai is declining to the point of malnutrition, particularly in children, and without cultivating some maize, the Maasai will not be able to survive in the Ngorongoro Conservation Area.

The future for the Maasai will very likely see major changes in both their economic system of land use and social relations of production. Many of these changes have already begun. The Maasai have increasingly integrated into the cash market, selling cattle to purchase grain, sugar, tea, and cloth. Many Maasai are taking up cultivation, particularly of maize (corn) to supplement losses in the livestock. Maasai have also experienced some benefits by these changes. Some local groups, particularly those living near the game parks, receive a portion of the park fees and hotel profits or are given jobs as drivers, scouts, and tour guides. Increasingly the Maasai have sent their children to public schools. School leavers have entered wage employment in tourism, police and military, livestock marketing, and professional jobs through secondary and post secondary education.

The increased commercial activity in Maasailand is leading to more polarization between rich and poor Maasai, with a wealthy few able to purchase land titles and cattle, and many poor and landless Maasai ending up as herding laborers or migrants to urban areas. Women in particular are at risk, migrating to towns like Namanga on the Kenya-Tanzania border engaging in prostitution and beer-brewing as the only sources of income.

THE TURKANA: FAMINE RELIEF

In contrast to the Maasai who have been strongly affected by commercial development, the Turkana remain the most isolated and mobile of all Kenya's pastoralists. Turkana district has been the target of some of the largest famine-relief efforts in Africa, as well as the location of Kenya's largest refugee camp at Kakuma, which numbers over 80,000 people. The majority of Turkana who still herd animals have faced increasing violence as Pokot raiders from the south and Ngoroko (bandit Turkana) raiders from the north attack with automatic weapons to steal cattle and camels.

The Turkana number over 400,000 people and inhabit a grazing environment 67,000 km^2, consisting mainly of scrub bush land and semi-desert in northwestern Kenya's Turkana District. The Turkana District is a low-lying plain in the Great Rift Valley between 660 and 900 m above sea level and with very low ecological potential due to erratic and low rainfall. Lying on Kenya's northwest border with Uganda and Sudan, Turkana is the most isolated and least developed district in the country.

The Turkana are part of a larger group of peoples in Sudan and Uganda that includes Karimojong, Dodos, Toposa, Teso, and Jie. In the 1800s, Turkana pushed into northwestern Kenya, driving away Rendille, Samburu, and Uas Ngishu Maasai with their large warrior-age regiments led by their prophet-diviner Lokerio. Following the death of Lokerio in 1880, the Turkana lost their momentum. Opposition to the British helped consolidate the Turkana in a series of wars between 1905 and 1920, where in one large battle 407 Turkana were killed and 19,000 cattle confiscated. Turkana were restricted by the British to Turkana District, a region so neglected and isolated that the area served as a prison for political prisoners including Jomo Kenyatta and other liberation activists during the 1950s.

Today, most Turkana are highly nomadic and decentralized, living in small household units (*awi*) consisting primarily of a male stock owner and his polygynous family. These autonomous households are affiliated into one of nineteen territorial sections, providing safe and extensive environments for grazing and watering livestock.

The essential pastoral strategy of the Turkana stock owner is to subdivide his herds and his family and move them to places where resources are temporarily available. During the brief rainy seasons, neighborhoods of households and herds are congregated in the lowland plains. These households separate during the dry season, with the women and children of the *awi* remaining with the milk camels and small stock in the plains, while the non-milk animals are dispersed into mobile satellite camps of age- and species-specific stock managed by adolescents and adult males. Long-term studies of the Ngisonyoka Turkana by the South Turkana Ecosystem Project shows the high degree of Turkana nomadism, where the *awi* moves from five to ten times a year in distances ranging from one to twenty kilometers (and occasionally up to fifty kilometers) in search of grazing and water for their livestock.

Turkana District remained as neglected under Kenyatta's government as under the British, and continues so to this day, despite large efforts by international development agencies, such as Norwegian aid (NORAD) who constructed a paved road to Lodwar in the 1980s. Famine, and the influx of famine-relief agencies, played a major role in Turkana District during the 1980s. Following the drought of 1980, where nearly one half of the district's population sought famine-relief as over 90% of their cattle, 40% of the camels, and 80% of their small stock died. The government of Kenya and members of the European Economic Community, particularly The Netherlands, Norway, and Germany, established the multi-million dollar Turkana Rehabilitation Project (TRP). By 1982 TRP was providing 180,000 kg of famine grains per week to 80,000 Turkana, creating eight large famine camps attracting pastoralists who quickly overgrazed the limited pasturage. The 1984–1985 famine which ravaged northeastern Africa went largely unnoticed in Turkana due to the long-standing famine-relief efforts in the district.

Seeking to reduce food dependency, TRP initiated several alternative subsistence schemes including small-scale irrigation schemes to settle destitute pastoralists, and Norway's disastrous attempt to build a fish processing plant on Lake Turkana. A Food for Work (FFW) program was initiated that contributed paid labor to ongoing irrigation, rural road-building, and tree-planting projects in the District. By 1985, only 15,000 Turkana were receiving famine-relief, although one-third of the district's pastoralists remained in or near the famine camps.

Anthropologist J. Terrence McCabe (1988, p. 17) summarizes the effects for the Turkana of settling around the camps:

> There is little hope for families who have settled in the famine camps to return to their former life.... The longer a herd-owner remains in a famine camp the weaker his bonds become with the pastoralist community. His "safety net" becomes the government and the international donor agencies rather than his fellow pastoralists.

In the 1990s, Turkana District became home to thousands of political refugees escaping wars in surrounding countries. In April 1991, Somalia's president Siad Barre was overthrown leading to intense inter-clan fighting; and in May 1991 the Ethiopian dictator Mengistu Haile Mariam was overthrown by a coalition of Eritrean and anti-Mengistu Ethiopians leading to a large influx of Somalis and Ethiopians into northern and northeastern Kenya. The civil war in Sudan between the non-Muslim south and the Muslim north, which had been going on since 1983, led to tens of thousands of Sudanese refugees, mainly Nuer and Dinka people, into northwest Kenya. Where the United Nations High Commission on Refugees (UNHCR) established 17 camps in the early 1990s in Kenya, by 2000 these had been consolidated (at Kenya's request) into two large camps at Kakuma in Turkana District and DaDaab in Wajir District near Somalia, the country's most desolate regions. Today Kakuma camp is home to 80,000 refugees from a dozen countries including Congo, Rwanda, and Sudan. It is the biggest city in Turkana District, and with 4200 people per km^2 (compared to the normal Turkana density of 7/km^2), is creating ecological havoc on an area with limited water and firewood. But it is also a lively city, with restaurants, dental offices, and shops run by enterprising refugees, providing jobs and livestock markets for many Turkana who have moved there. But the camp has also placed great demands on the District, with little benefit going to Turkana in the rest of the district.

The greatest risks to Turkana in recent times have been the cattle raids of heavily armed Pokot, pastoral neighbors to their south, who have raided cattle without fear of punishment due to their protection by then President Moi. In addition, Turkana face raids from northern Turkana who have acquired automatic weapons from southern Sudan guerrillas. These Ngoroko (bandits) have also raided Samburu and Ariaal, where following an attack in December 1996, the Turkana shot down a pursuing military helicopter, killing the Samburu District Commissioner. This led to retaliation by the Kenyan government with fighter planes against Turkana camps, many of whom had nothing to do with the raids. Clearly the situations of drought, famine, refugees, and raids have taken a toll on Turkana herders and their ability to survive in this precarious environment.

THE RENDILLE: PASTORALISM AND DROUGHT IN THE KAISUT DESERT

The Rendille are a pastoral population of 25,000 living in the Kaisut Desert of Marsabit District, Kenya, between Lake Turkana and Mt. Marsabit. They are among the oldest and conservative pastoral groups in East Africa, Afro-Asiatic speakers who probably descend from the same Cushitic peoples as present day Somalis, although the Rendille do not practice Islam but have their own beliefs and religion. Always a small population, Rendille maintain a specialized camel and small stock pastoralism adapted to their desert environment, although recently they have begun to acquire cattle from their Ariaal neighbors and relatives. In former times, the Rendille occupied lands from present day Turkana District in the northwest to much of north central Kenya. But Boran cattle pastoralists and Gabra camel pastoralists moved into Rendille lands from Ethiopia after the sixteenth century, and the expanding Turkana pushed Rendille and their allies the Samburu from west of Lake Turkana to the Rendille's present day location in Marsabit District. The Rendille have had an alliance with the Maa-speaking Samburu for several centuries, where surplus women from the monogamous Rendille are taken as second wives by Samburu, and where Ariaal resulted from the union of these two larger groups. It is likely that the Samburu and Maasai age-set system as well as their practices of male and female circumcision were acquired from the Rendille, for other Nilotic groups from whom the Maasai descend, including Turkana, do not practice these customs.

Marsabit District is Kenya's largest but least populated area, annual rainfall is less than 250mm in the lowlands and 800mm in the highlands of Mt. Marsabit and the Ndoto Mountains. Unlike the Turkana who live in small mobile homesteads, the Rendille typically live in large semi-nomadic settlements of 50 houses or more with large herds of camels and small stock. The large village size, shared by the Ariaal, probably developed as a defensive strategy against enemy raiders. Camels are the basis of Rendille life, and they are rarely sold or traded. In the wet season, one camel provides ten liters of milk daily, which constitutes 70% of their wet-season calories. In the dry season, Rendille depend on slaughtered goats and the trade of small stock for grains, tea, and sugar. In the last century, Rendille traded livestock for grains from the agricultural Konso and Dasenech of Ethiopia.

Under British colonial rule, northern Kenyan pastoralists including Rendille, Samburu, Turkana, and Boran were confined to specific "tribal grazing areas" and prohibited from moving onto other group's lands. Many older Rendille today assert that the colonial boundary controls reduced the raiding and periodic killings over water and pasture, events which have re-emerged today. Nevertheless, the Rendille herding range was reduced from 57,600 km^2 to 8000 km^2 while their human population grew from about 8000 to 25,000 between 1960 and 2000.

Following the droughts of 1968–1973, many Rendille began to settle near small trading towns and police posts in Marsabit District including Laisamis, Archer's Post, and Marsabit town. Catholic and Protestant missions began long-term famine distribution efforts and agricultural schemes for destitute nomads, creating "famine-relief towns" in the Kaisut Desert at watering holes at Kargi and Korr, and agricultural settlements on Marsabit Mountain at Nasikakwe and

Songa. In the last fifteen years, these small towns have grown dramatically, and today about 30% of the Rendille population are permanently settled. Marsabit town, the district capital, is now 30,000 people, six times its population in 1975.

While the majority of Rendille continue to live as pastoralists raising camels and small stocks many settled near towns on a permanent basis. Although they still own substantial numbers of animals, livestock are not kept in the village as in former times, but are herded in distant camps called *fora*. Consequently these settled Rendille have shifted their diet from protein rich camel's milk to protein poor *posho* meal. The move to settle is prompted by many factors, including loss of livestock during drought and political insecurity from raids by neighboring Gabra, Turkana, and Somalis during the 1980s and 1990s. But Rendille have also been lured to towns by Christian missions offering famine relief foods, schools, and dispensaries, and although they have not abandoned pastoralism, prefer to settle than move with the animals. The Ariaal are different in this respect, where many communities continue to live with their camels, cattle, and small stock.

From 1975–1985, the Rendille and Ariaal became targets of a large multilateral project, UNESCO's Integrated Project in Arid Lands (IPAL), which emerged following the Conference on Desertification held in Nairobi by the newly created United Nations Environment Program's (UNEP) and UNESCO's Man and the Biosphere Programme. "Desertification" emerged as a concept in scientific discussions following the Sahelian Famine (1968–1976) in West Africa, which embraced the view that deserts were expanding mainly because of human mismanagement of the rangeland. The IPAL project intended to combine basic research in land use with practical policies aimed at reducing environmental degradation. Its first proposed field station (out of several world wide) was Marsabit District, and IPAL chose Rendille, Ariaal, and Gabra as subjects to demonstrate human/environment interaction.

Because IPAL viewed pastoral practices as responsible for overgrazing in areas such as Korr and Kargi towns (when in fact people settled there in search of famine foods), IPAL implemented projects aimed at reducing herd size by encouraging more livestock marketing as well as improving livestock production by building roads, water catchments, and improving veterinary care. Despite these measures, Rendille did not increase their livestock offtake (marketing or butchering), and continued to sell animals only during dry seasons to purchase grains when milk supplies ran low. By 1985, the IPAL project had disbanded, most international development efforts concentrated on improving agricultural crop production on Mt. Marsabit rather than pastoralism as the key to improving the region's economy.

The effects of the church-sponsored famine-relief projects on the Rendille have been large. Accustomed to receiving famine relief foods during the droughts of the 1970s and 1980s, many Rendille permanently moved to the famine-relief towns of Korr and Kargi, created largely by the Catholic Church. Here, Rendille live in their traditional circle of houses, but no animals are to be found. Rather, their camels and small stock are herded in distant *fora* camps by warriors and boys, while settlements of older men, women, and younger children subsist off of mission handouts or grains purchased with sales of their diminishing livestock herds. GTZ (the German Development Corporation) noted in a 1994 workshop that the Rendille have become too used to charity and were too ready to accept aid without seeking new forms of income. While there may be some truth to this, the Rendille are also in a difficult position of being surrounded by other competing pastoral groups—Boran, Gabra, Samburu, and Somali—and find themselves in an increasingly restricted herding environment. Furthermore, Rendille have sought new ways to continue their pastoral economy, including digging new water wells near the towns so they can keep animals in residence, at least during the wet season when there is sufficient grazing for their livestock.

While the pastoral systems of Maasai, Turkana, and Rendille have been greatly affected by the recent challenges of population growth, restriction of herding range, drought, famine, political insecurity and ethnic conflict, these populations continue to rely on their animals for their basic economic needs of food and income. Despite these problems, pastoralism remains one of the few methods by which these people can wrest food and livelihood from Kenya's arid regions. For pastoralism to continue, however, there must be changes in both pastoral practices as well as the policies of national governments and international development agencies aimed at pastoral peoples. These recommendations are discussed in the final chapter.

3

Ariaal Identity and Culture

It is not known how long the Ariaal have existed as a distinct social grouping, although mixed communities of Samburu and Rendille are known to have lived in their current locations near the Ndoto Mountains and Mt. Marsabit since at least the nineteenth century. Ariaal elders spoke to me of their great grandfathers who lived along the Milgis and Merille Rivers (near present-day Laisamis) during the time the Kipeko age-set (circa 1838–1850) were warriors, while Samburu elders in the 1950s described to the anthropologist Paul Spencer how Samburu and Rendille intermarried and fought wars against Turkana, Boran, and Maasai since at least the Kipayang age-set were warriors (c. 1823–1837).

Paul Spencer was the first to describe the Samburu–Rendille relationship in his book *Nomads in Alliance*. He argued that the two culturally distinct societies, the Samburu cattle keepers of the western highlands and the Rendille camel keepers of the arid lowlands, allied and intermarried based on the noncompetitiveness of their herding environments. Furthermore, Spencer showed how the Ariaal formed as a cultural bridge between the two larger groups, as poor Rendille, unable to inherit their fathers' camel herds due to rules of primogeniture (inheritance by oldest son), took up cattle and small stock herding with Samburu-speaking groups, while Samburu took Rendille women as second or third wives. The Ariaal emerged as a mixed group, bilingual in Samburu and Rendille, and keeping cattle as well as camels and small stock on the boundary between the two larger groups.

Most Ariaal families today trace their origins to immigrants from Rendille and Samburu, but many families described ancestors that migrated from Laikipiak Maasai, Boran, Turkana, Somali, Meru, and Dasenech tribes. While distinct ethnic groups based on language and culture certainly exist, the concept of "tribal" identities was to a large extent created by colonial rulers to facilitate their administration and control. While the administrative boundaries of Samburu, Turkana, and Marsabit Districts were drawn to separate groups, the line between "tribes" is much more ambiguous. The Ariaal are a distinct case in point.

Located along a topographical interface that divides highland Samburu District from lowland Marsabit District, Ariaal live in large semi-sedentary settlements with their milk animals and small stock, sending most of their non-milking cattle and camels to mobile herding camps managed by warriors and adolescent boys. Normally cattle and camels are not herded together, as cattle eat grass and need watering every 2–3 days, while camels can survive for almost two weeks without watering, eating the twigs and leaves of bushes spread out in the desert environment. The Ariaal are able to raise both types of large animals, as well as small stock who also need frequent watering, by living between highland and lowland resources along the base of the Ndoto Mountains and the hills of Mt. Marsabit. Some Ariaal live exclusively with their cattle in the highlands, strongly resembling Samburu in house and settlement structure, others live with their camels in large Rendille-type settlements in the lowlands. Nearly all Ariaal, however, own mixed herds of camels, cattle, and small stock, although some may be loaned or kept elsewhere. Ariaal livestock management is described more fully in Chapter 4.

ORIGINS OF THE ARIAAL

Kenya is a great melting pot of cultures, the results of successive waves of immigration from different parts of the African continent. Archeological evidence shows specialized cattle-keeping pastoralism in East Africa 4000 years ago, while linguistic evidence suggests these herders may originally be from Ethiopia where Cushitic languages are spoken. Cushitic speaking farmers lived in Tanzania 3000 years ago, while Nilotic-speaking agro-pastoralists entered Kenya from Sudan about 2000 years ago, about the same time that Bantu-speaking farmers from West and Central Africa reached the Indian Ocean coast.

Within the last 1000 years, Nilotes speaking the Maa (Maasai related) languages moved south from Sudan into Kenya's broad grasslands and savannas, linguistically separating by 1600 A.D. into northern (Samburu, Chamus, and Parakuyu), central (Laikipiak Maasai), western (Uasin Gishu Maasai), and southern Maa speaking groups including the main Maasai groups of Kaputei, Loita, Purko, and Kisongo Maasai. Unlike other Nilotes such as Turkana who do not circumcise their men and women, Maa speakers mingled with Cushitic pastoralists and adopted the customs of male and female circumcision and named age-sets.

By 1800 A.D. most of the savannas and arid plains of Kenya were populated by nomadic pastoralists, with agriculturalists located mainly around Lake Victoria, Mt. Kenya, Mt. Kilimanjaro, and the Indian Ocean coast. Southern Maasai groups occupied the grasslands of central and southern Kenya, while Laikipiak and Uasin Gishu Maasai (now extinct) as well as Samburu and LChamus people raised cattle and small stock in the Rift Valley region around Lake Baringo. A variety of Kalenjin speakers (Nilotes distantly related to Maasai, including Nandi and Kipsigis) mixed cattle keeping and horticulture in the western highlands, while cattle-keeping Turkana and Boran and camel-keeping Rendille, Gabra, and Somalis, practiced more specialized animal pastoralism in the dry north.

During the mid-nineteenth century many of these pastoral populations competed for grazing lands. The Turkana expelled Samburu and Rendille from the northern plains west of Lake Turkana, while Samburu pushed Laikipiak off the Leroki Plateau and Marsabit Mountain and Boran off Mt. Nyiru. To the south, rival Maasai tribes competed for the rich grazing lands around the Rift Valley Lakes Naivasha and Nakuru, with the southern Maasai ultimately defeating and dispersing Laikipiak and Uasin Gishu Maasai from Kenya's central plains. Maasai traditions hold that a Purko *laibon* (medicine man) Mbatiany persuaded the warriors from the Kisongo Maasai to join the Purko and deal the Laikipiak a total defeat. The Laikipiak were destroyed, and their few survivors assimilated into neighboring Samburu, LChamus, Turkana, and the newly emerging Ariaal communities.

The Samburu and Rendille were only marginally involved in the Laikipiak wars to the south, although they fought against Laikipiak around Mt. Marsabit and the present town of Laisamis, whose name (in Maa) means the "place of the bad smells" from the human carnage.

By 1875, the Samburu had moved away from Turkana raiders and were living on the eastern side of Lake Turkana, while their Rendille allies near Mt. Marsabit fought Laikipiak Maasai who had fled the Purko Maasai in the south. It is during the warriorhood of the Tarigirik age-set (1866–1880) that Ariaal are first distinguished from the Rendille in contemporary oral histories, and they are noted for their fierce fighting against the Laikipiak, from whom Ariaal captured a large number of camels and built up their herds in a significant way. Ariaal families from Lorokushu clan on Marsabit Mountain say they were living on the mountain during the Kiteku age-set (c. 1838–1852) and fought Laikipiak Maasai when the Marikon age-set were warriors (c. 1880–1894). Ariaal age-sets names are listed in Table 3.1.

Kenyan pastoralists faced hardship not only from the warfare of the latter nineteenth century but also from the steady series of diseases, including bovine pleuro-pneumonia in 1882 and rinderpest in 1891 and 1898 (which swept from Egypt to South Africa, devastating cattle herds throughout

TABLE 3.1 SAMBURU, ARIAAL, AND RENDILLE AGE-SET CHRONOLOGY: AGE-SETS AND INITIATION YEAR

Samburu		Ariaal		Rendille	
		Meishopo	c.1781		
		Kurukua	c.1795		
		Petaa	c.1809		
Kipayang	c.1823	Kipayang	c.1824		
Kipeko	c.1837	Kipeko	c.1838	Kipeko	c.1839
Kiteku	c.1851	Kiteku	c.1852	Libaale	c.1853
Tarigirik	c.1865	Tarigirik	c.1866	Dibgudo	c.1867
Merikon	c.1879	Merikon	c.1880	Dismala	c.1881
Terito	c.1893	Terito	c.1894	Irbangudo	1895
Merisho	1912 (delayed)	Merisho	1910	Difgudo	1910
Kiliako	1921	Kiliako	1922	Irbaalis	1923
Mekuri	1936	Mekuri	1937	Libaale	1937
Kimaniki	1948	Kimaniki	1951	Irbandif	1951
Kishili	1962	Kishili	1964	Difgudo	1965
Kororo	1976	Kororo	1978	Irbangudo	1979
Moli	1990	Moli	1992	Moli	1993

Sources: Schlee 1989, p. 76; Sobania 1980, p. 135; Spencer 1973, pp. 150–165 for Samburu and Rendille; for Ariaal, Fratkin interviews with Kordidi Leaduma, Marsabit, July 1996.

East Africa), followed by smallpox which reappeared during drought and famines of the 1890s. Where rinderpest and pneumonia had wiped out Maasai, Turkana, and Samburu cattle herds, Rendille camels had escaped unharmed. W. A. Chanler, a European adventurer traveling through Rendille territory in 1892–1893, reported that the Rendille were the only prosperous pastoralists he encountered, while the Samburu he met along the eastern side of the Ndoto Mountains were destitute and eager to exchange donkeys and small stock for cattle, of which they possessed very few.

My adopted Ariaal father, Lekati Leaduma, himself descended from Laikipiak Maasai, described this period:

During the times of Terito age-set [c. 1894–1910] after the period of warfare with the Maasai, all the

Samburu were living on this side of the Ndoto Mountains. Even my father was living on Marsabit Mountain, helping herd camels and cattle. During this time, and of the Merikon age-set [1880–1894] before them, Samburu were poor. When the cattle were finished (by rinderpest), Samburu were living as *Dorrobo* [poor hunters-gatherers], even eating elephants. Some stole camels from Rendille as thieves (*tombon*), others worked for the Rendille as herd-boys, to be paid in small stock, camels, or cattle.

During the last decade of the nineteenth century, poor Samburu migrated toward Rendille and formed mixed Samburu/Rendille communities of impoverished herders attempting to build up small stock, camels, and cattle near the mountain bases. These groups were alternatively called *Masagera* (meaning roughly "those Rendille who follow Maasai" in Samburu), *Turia* (Samburu for "mixture"), or *Ariaal*. The term Ariaal may derive from the Boran word for mobile livestock camp (*arjara*), and denoted in the first half of this century those mixed groups of Rendille, Boran, and Samburu who moved with their animals along the mountain bases.

By the end of the nineteenth century, the fortunes of the Samburu and the Rendille dramatically reversed. Where the Samburu and Ariaal steadily rebuilt their herds, the spread of smallpox to the Marsabit District devastated the Rendille to a greater degree than the Samburu, who possibly gained immunity from previous contact with Swahili caravans that bypassed the more isolated Rendille. Concentrated in large populations in the Chalbi and Kaisut Deserts, the Rendille lost one-half of their population to smallpox.

By 1900, the former position of strength and superiority of the Rendille in their alliance with the Samburu was lost. The Rendille had large camel herds but few herders to manage them, and they hired and adopted Samburu and Ariaal labor in exchange for livestock. The Rendille's misfortunes thus became both the Samburu and Ariaal's good fortune, as they were able to build their cattle and small stock herds at a steady rate.

During British colonial rule, the government had little use for the arid deserts of the northern half of the country, but utilized it as a military buffer against the expanding Ethiopian empire of Menelik II as well as French and Italian rivals. Lord Delamere, one of the founding British settlers in Kenya, journeyed through Marsabit in 1897, and, sensing its usefulness to the Kenya colony, encouraged its incorporation and later administration as the Northern Frontier District (NFD).

An Ariaal elder from Karare village on Marsabit Mountain, Leruk of Lorokushu clan, told me how his uncle was the first to meet Lord Delamere. The British explorer was returning from the north near Ethiopia and rode up Mt. Marsabit on horseback, leading a detachment of armed British soldiers. The Ariaal warriors were also armed from raiding the Boran, and were ready to fight the whites, who they had never seen before. But a young warrior (Leruk, the uncle) approached Delamere with a handful of grass, the sign of peace. Delamere also pulled up some grass, and the two embraced. Delamere offered Leruk a rifle, and Leruk gave him a cow, after which the Ariaal got along peaceably with the British. Unlike the Turkana or Nandi, who periodically fought with the British administration, the Ariaal, Samburu, and Rendille welcomed the creation of administrative police posts in Marsabit as a means of protection against enemy Turkana and Boran pastoralists. The Samburu, in particular, began a tradition of enlisting in the colonial police and military, where during World War II, 348 Samburu warriors (over 20% of the entire warrior age-grade) enlisted in the King's African Rifles to fight overseas. Later, Samburu continued to serve in the Administrative Police and were used to track Kikuyu guerrillas during the Mau Mau rebellion of the 1950s.

The Rendille remained more isolated than the Samburu in dealings with the colonial government, but they were nevertheless affected by British colonial policies, particularly those maintaining tribal grazing controls. They were prohibited from burning grasses on Marsabit Mountain, which had enabled them to graze camels by killing ticks and other parasites, and the British allowed Boran to bring their cattle on the mountain. The Boran, originally from southern Ethiopia, have grazed their animals in northern Kenya since at least the mid-nineteenth century. Many Boran migrated to Marsabit Mountain from the north as well as Wajir District to the east in the 1930s to work on the colonial road being built from Nairobi to Moyale on the Ethiopian border.

I asked Lugi Lengesen why the British had encouraged the Boran to settle on Marsabit Mountain, given even the colonial administration's descriptions of the Boran as "troublesome" and the Rendille as "cooperative and law abiding." Lugi replied with a chuckle, "they didn't like camels' milk in their tea, so they invited the Boran and their cattle to the mountain!"

During the *shifta* war in the 1960s, a large battle was fought between armed Boran/Somali and Ariaal warriors living near Baiyo Mountain, not far from where the Lewogoso settlement presently lies. At last fifty raiders were killed, while Ariaal lost three people. Kitoip Lenkiribe, who was then a young warrior (Kishili age-set) from Lewogoso settlement, described the battle:

> The raiders came to steal our animals, which were watering near Baiyo [Mountain] by the Milgis [River] at Larapasie. Some girls who were herding ran to the village saying how *shifta* had taken their goats and were feasting on them. Our warriors ran to meet the enemy, with warriors coming also from Longieli [another Ariaal settlement] nearby. There were several hundred *shifta*, and probably sixty of our warriors. The fighting lasted all day and into the night. Although they had rifles, we were able to creep up on them in the dark and attack with our spears. When our spears were finished [i.e., thrown], we ran and attacked with our *rungus* [clubs] and swords. Some of us even bent our swords and threw them like clubs, cutting them in the neck. The Boran are frightened to fight at night, but we aren't. They were wearing their white hats, so they were easy to see. We killed many people. Some Boran grabbed us

by the legs, begging us not to kill them. Those we
didn't kill, ran off. The army came the next day in a
lorry to hunt them down, but we had to hunt them
down on foot.

By 1969, *shifta* resistance had deteriorated into sporadic
livestock raids against Ariaal and Rendille Samburu settlements. The Ariaal and Rendille have remained enemies
with Boran, and raids between these groups (as well as
against Turkana) continue to this day.

ARIAAL IDENTITY

Ariaal have borrowed customs from both Samburu and Rendille cultures and have formed a "bridge culture" in the process. In many ways, Samburu and Rendille cultures strongly
resemble each other. Both societies are organized by segmentary descent organization, a decentralized political system
based on the autonomy of related groups organized into
families, lineages, and clans. In some situations clans will act
together, in others they act separately. While never reaching
the fratricidal level of the recent Somali civil war, segmentary descent organization operates similarly in Samburu and
Rendille as there is no clearly defined position of centralized
leadership. Nevertheless, elders strive for peaceful relations
between the clans and try to reach consensus in most political matters.

In addition to segmentary descent organization, both
Samburu and Rendille have age-set organizations where
young men from all clans are initiated into named age-sets
(recruited, in the Samburu and Rendille cases, every fourteen years) who move collectively through the age-grade
ladder of "boy," "warrior," and "elder."

Despite the similarities in age-set and descent group organization, the Samburu and Rendille are very distinct societies. The Samburu are closely related to the pastoral Maasai
and share many customs with other Nilotes (from Sudan)
including beliefs in diviner-prophets, the power of sorcery,
shared origin stories, and strong personal attachments to

their cattle reflected in songs, stories, material arts, and ritual feasting. The Rendille, on the other hand, are Cushitic speakers from Africa's Horn and share camel-keeping customs with related Somali and Gabra peoples. This tradition includes weekly, lunar, annual, and seven year calendars (following the named days of the week) which organize the timing of periodic ceremonies blessing livestock (particularly camels) and the initiation of age-sets. They also share customs of male and female circumcision, which are borrowed by the Samburu and Maasai but not other Nilotes such as Turkana.

The Ariaal lie "betwixt and between" these two larger Nilotic and Cushitic traditions. Most Ariaal are bilingual in Samburu and Rendille, although men prefer to speak in Samburu, while Samburu and Rendille are largely monolingual. Schlee (1989) observes that Ariaal men have only rudimentary knowledge of Rendille. Ariaal settlements range from small Samburu-type homesteads keeping mainly cattle in the highlands to large Rendille-type settlements in the lowlands keeping large herds of camels and small stock. Ariaal consider themselves more Samburu than Rendille owing to their incorporation into Samburu clans, their following Samburu age-set rituals including the *mugit* ox-slaughters, and their preference for Samburu language; but Ariaal also follow Rendille customs of annual camel blessings and evening prayers by elders in the *naabo* ritual center of each Ariaal village, ceremonies not found in Samburu communities.

The settlement's ritual center, the *naabo*, is a small circle about five yards wide, surrounded by a thorn bush fence and containing a small fire that is kept burning every day. Men gather here every night for evening prayers, and conduct the seasonal rituals of *sorio* and *almodo* discussed below. In their prayers, the elders thank God (*N'gai*) for life. As one elder leads the blessings, the other men affirm God's name in unison, opening and closing their hands in supplication:

May God bless everything (*N'gai!*)
May God bless those with hair (warriors) and those without (*N'gai!*)

May God bless those in the bush and those who are at home (*N'gai!*)

May god give us both boys and girls (*N'gai!*)

May God look after the camels (*N'gai!*)

May God look after the cattle (*N'gai!*)

May God look after us all (*N'gai!*)

May we have peace in the land (*N'gai!*)

God says Yes! (*Etejo n'gai aiya!*)

ARIAAL CLAN SETTLEMENTS

Ariaal settlements are local descent groups belonging to the larger Samburu system, where communities are made up of relatives from the same clan. The Samburu descent group system divides the society into two halves (or moieties), the White Cattle and Black Cattle. Each moiety is made up of four clans (*l-marei*, the "ribs"), with the White Cattle clans of *Lukumai, Lorokushu, Longieli;* and *Loimusi* (the latter not represented in Ariaal), and the Black Cattle clans of *Masala, Pisikishu* (*Turia* in Ariaal), *Nyaparai* (*LeSarge* in Ariaal), and *Lng'wesi* (the latter clan is not found in Ariaal). The largest clans in Ariaal are Lorokushu, Lukumai, Longieli, Masala, and Turia.

There are approximately twenty-five Ariaal clan settlements, located in the southwestern part of the Marsabit District and on Marsabit Mountain. The majority of the camel-keeping Ariaal settlements (including Lewogoso Lukumai) are located at the base of the Ndoto Mountains between Ngurunit and Laisamis towns, while the cattle-keeping settlements are found in the highland regions of the Ndotos and Mt. Marsabit.

Each clan (and the larger clan settlements) are made up of several subclans (usually two to three per clan), each of which is made up of distinct lineages, groups of families whose members can trace a common ancestor, usually to the grandparent level. An example is the Lengesen lineage (to which my friend Lugi belongs), which is part of Lewogoso subclan of the Lukumai clan of White Cattle moiety of Samburu (and

Ariaal). While lineages and subclans are exogamous (members cannot marry each other), clans are not. One hundred years ago when the society was much smaller, Ariaal clans were probably the size of subclans today and were more exogamous.

Clan and sub-clan identity is the most important category of Ariaal life. When a person meets another Samburu or Ariaal or Rendille, the first question one asks is "*Leng'ai era?*"—from which clan (or *nkang*/village) are you? If one can establish a kinship tie based on descent or marriage, that person is usually welcomed into the community, and often given a place to stay and food to eat. The second most important identity is age-set membership, where any age-mate (a member of your age-set) is offered shelter and food from another age-mate, no matter what the kinship identity. Today when I visit Ariaal villages, I greet men my age by the proper *Sopa! Murrata* (Greetings, fellow warrior), often to the grin and amazement of the stranger I approach.

Ariaal settlements are typically composed of members of the same patrilineal subclan. Large settlements like Lewogoso Lukumai consist of several lineages or family groupings of families sharing the same name (i.e., Lengesen) and common ancestor, smaller settlements as in the highlands are usually members of one lineage or sublineage grouping (i.e., two brothers and their families). Where men in a subclan settlement are typically brothers or fathers and sons, married women come from other subclan settlements and will remain in their husband's community even after his death. Sons, when they marry, bring their brides to their own subclan village, while daughters are married out to men from other clan settlements. Although subclans are exogamous, Ariaal warriors can "bead" girlfriends from the same subclan, but not from the same lineage, as sexual relations would be incestuous at that level.

Clan and moiety level affiliation are not very important in day-to-day life, but they are important in organizing age-set rituals, which are undertaken collectively by members of the same clan. Subclans are more important because they are the basis of shared residence, cooperative herding, and mutual defense of the village against human enemies and predators such as lions attacking their livestock. The clan settlement of Lewogoso, described in more detail in Chapter 5, is fairly isolated, located twenty miles from the next clan settlement of Longieli. Moreover, warriors from different subclan settlements are usually hostile to one another (usually arising over fights about girlfriends), but in typical segmentary descent fashion, will readily unite to fight a common enemy, such as Turkana.

AGE-GRADES AND AGE-SET ORGANIZATION

Outside of kinship ties of descent and marriage, the most important social category is that of age grades and age sets. This social organization is extremely important to many pastoral groups of East Africa, including Maasai, Samburu, and Rendille. Boran and Turkana also categorize men by generation or age grade, but do not have named age-sets. Age-grades are distinct stages of life marked by prescribed (necessary and expected) sets of behaviors for members sharing the same stage in the life cycle. For males the distinct age grades are boys (*laiyeni, laiyok*), warriors (*lmurran, lmurrani*), and elders (*lpayien, lpayieni*); although women are not formally initiated into age sets, they too pass through distinct life stages as young girls (*ntito, ntoyie*), adolescent girls (*naikira, naikiran*), and married women (*nparatut, nparatuti*). Each age grade has explicit rules about what clothes and ornaments one may wear, what foods one may eat, and with whom one may share food, lodging, or association. For example, adolescent boys and married elders may milk camels, but married women or warriors may not; warriors may wear red ochre in their hair, grow their hair, and wear ivory (or today white plastic) earrings, but boys may not. Warriors may not eat food that women have seen, touched, or prepared. Adolescent girls should not sleep in the same house as their fathers, and while they may have sex with warriors, they may never have sex with a married man. Similarly, warriors should not have sex with married women (although they sometimes do, particularly if it is their former girlfriend).

Age-sets are a related but different entity than age grades. Men are initiated in particular and named age-sets when they are circumcised at early adolescence. They remain members of this age set for life, passing through the ladder of different age-grades together as warriors, junior elders, and senior elders. Like Rendille and Samburu, Ariaal age-sets are initiated every fourteen years, when boys who are three sets below that of their fathers, usually between the ages of ten and twenty-five, are circumcised with other members of their clan. For the next fourteen years, the warriors are expected to herd animals in the distant camps and protect the settlements from armed attack. Two years before the initiation of the next warrior age set, these men are released from warriorhood and allowed to marry and start families of their own.

Warriorhood is perhaps the most important period in a man's life. Young boys look up to the warriors and long to be initiated themselves, adolescent girls compose songs and bead jewelry for their warrior lovers, mothers pray for the warriors safety. Old men, sitting in the shade playing the *mbau* board game, talk about their days as warriors and admonish the behavior of warriors today, like old veterans in the VFW in our towns. It is difficult not to be impressed by the sight of several warriors, resplendent in their long red-dyed braids of hair, adorned with multicolored armbands and necklaces, carrying spears and wearing long swords.

For Ariaal men, circumcision and initiation into warriorhood is the most important event of their life. The circumcision ritual is performed in specially constructed villages outside the larger clan settlement, where the mother of each initiate builds her house for the two months of the circumcision village's existence. The circumcision operation is performed by a man from the Dorrobo tribe, who moves from boy to boy outside his mother's house in the circle. Two male relatives hold the youth's back and right leg while the operation is performed. An initiate should not flinch or shout out during the operation, or he will be shamed for life. The boys rest in the circumcision village for about a month, until they have healed.

During their fourteen-year period as warriors, the young men perform a series of ox slaughters called *mugit*, large ceremonies performed with their clan groups. At each *mugit* ceremony, warriors build a settlement outside their clan villages, making small houses for each individual. Each warrior sacrifices an ox at the *mugit*, distributing the meat to his age-mates and to his relatives in the home settlement. The ritual lasts several days, as groups of three to four warriors kill their animals (in the bush), offering meat to the elders, and leaving meat for the women from the village to collect later in the day. Before feasting, the clan elders collectively address the warriors, emphasizing the need for warriors to act with respect toward the elders and the society at large. At the end of each *mugit*, the clan elders collectively bless the warriors.

The first *mugit* (the "*mugit* of the arrows") occurs a month after the circumcision ritual. It marks the point when initiates become junior warriors. At this point they must follow strict food prohibitions, never allowing women and especially their mothers to see the roasted meat they eat. The boys are allowed to put red ochre in their hair, which is beginning to grow out, and to wear the jewelry and red cloths of warriors. A second *mugit* is held the following month, the "*mugit* of the roasting sticks," where the age-set is divided into senior (right side) and junior (left side) divisions, separating the older from younger warriors. Five years later comes the "*mugit* of the name," signifying the maturation of the age-set as the clan elders give the age-set its name, and decide (in secret) who will be the ritual leader (*launon*) of the set for the entire clan. The *launon* should be a mature and responsible leader, avoiding fights and resolving internal disputes. He tours the country and builds up a herd of about 40 cattle from clan warriors, managing the herd in trust for the age-set. This *mugit* is repeated a month later, with each warrior again sacrificing an ox.

Five years after the "*mugit* of the name," the "*mugit* of the bull" is performed, after which the ritual leader, followed by his age-mates, can marry. The *launon* selects a bull from the collective herd, which he and his age-mates suffocate in the *mugit* settlement. A final ceremony, the *"mugit* of the milk and leaves," is performed after the ritual leader and the majority of his clan age-mates are married. On the evening before the first oxen are killed, the elders give the *murran* a final blessing inside the elder's ritual enclosure, and they all drink milk together. Following this last *mugit*, the warriors shave their heads, if they haven't already done so, and emerge as junior elders of the society.

The Rendille do not have *mugit* rites, but have large clan-based circumcision rituals (*khandi*) followed by a single and inclusive ceremony for all their warriors called the *gaalgulamme*, in which the age-set is given its name. The Ariaal are excluded from participating in *gaalgulamme*, as their clans are not considered part of the Rendille descent group organization.

Ariaal Religious Culture: Rites of Community, Rites of Affliction, and Rites of Passage

Like other East African pastoralists with segmentary descent organization, Ariaal religion is decentralized and autonomous. There is no ancestor worship nor any organization of priests or secret societies, features which are found in settled agricultural societies such as Bantu speakers of West Africa. The Ariaal do believe in a supreme being and creator, called *N'gai* in Samburu (*Wakh* in Rendille), who is appealed to in prayers for peace, rain, and fertility, but this creator is a distant force which is not directly concerned with affairs on earth.

Ariaal share the Samburu (and Maasai) origin myth that God led Maa-speaking people out of the Kerio Valley (in present-day Turkana District) by a knotted rope, giving cattle only to the Maa people (and making it perfectly legitimate to "take-back" the cattle of Turkana, Boran, and other groups). Views of an afterlife, however, are poorly defined and vague. I once asked an elderly Ariaal man "where do you go when you die?" and he replied in wide-eyed anticipation, "I don't know, do you?" When an individual dies, the body is taken far from the settlement deep into "the bush" and laid on the right side. If hyenas have not consumed the body by the following day, it is feared that a spirit will remain in the area, so a goat is slaughtered to attract scavengers. Exceptions to this procedure are small infants, who are buried in the household hearth, and important adults such as *laibons* who are buried in the settlement, after which the community moves to a new location. There is some belief in ghosts and spirits of the dead, particularly of people who died violently in warfare or attacks by lions, but there are no ancestors with distinct personalities who take a sharp interest in human affairs.

Certain Ariaal families are known as *lais* (pl. *laisi*) who possess powerful curses and who lead communitywide prayers, but they have no overt priestly roles. In general, it is the community of elders acting collectively who lead the community in prayers and blessings. If one accepts a definition that religion is an expression of human belief in (and need for) intervention by more powerful supernatural forces, then Ariaal are a religious people.

Victor Turner, who studied religion among the Ndembu of Zambia, distinguished three levels of public ritual activity in traditional society: *rites of community,* in which the entire community participates in periodic, seasonal or annual events such as planting or harvest rites or Sunday mass; *rites of passage,* which include public ceremonies noting changes in life status including birth, adolescence, marriage, and death rituals; and *rites of affliction,* which are rituals led by traditional healers that seek supernatural intervention to treat suffering believed to be caused by supernatural forces such as an ancestor's curse, witchcraft, or sorcery. All three types of rituals are found among the Ariaal.

Camel-keeping Ariaal (but not cattle-keeping communities) share with the Rendille periodic community rituals associated with the well being of camels. These include *almodo,* the annual blessing of livestock which initiates a new year, and *sorio* in which every household sacrifices a goat or sheep on four occasions each year. The Rendille share with Boran, Gabra, and Sakuye an elaborate calendar that includes a named seven-day week, a twenty-eight day lunar calendar, an annual year of 365 days (made up of fifty-two weeks and one day), and a seven-year cycle where each year is named after a day of the week [e.g., "Monday" (*Alasmin*) year, followed by "Tuesday" (*Talaata*) year, etc.] culminating in two seven-year cycles which lead to the initiation of new age-set every fourteen years.

Almodo is held over two weeks at the end of the fifty-two-week year, commencing on the day of the week corresponding with the name of the new year. *Almodo* occurs in April and May, at the times of the spring rains, and is a ceremony of renewal and blessing. It begins as women bring milk to the *naabo*, where the male elders give blessings and ask God to protect the village and its animals. The *naabo* blessings are repeated seven days later, this time with sour milk rather than fresh milk, and ends seven days later when all of the elders shave their heads and "wash" the settlement's livestock in milk (sprinkling milk on their backs or legs). This is followed by joyous processions through a ritual gateway (*ulukh*) located outside the village on its western side, first by the settlement's married women, followed by their animals, followed by the elders blowing *kudu* horns and shouting blessings. The gateway consists of two branches of thorn bush with a small fire lit on either side and two lambs tied to the gate. Two days later, the houses are disassembled, loaded on pack animals, and the whole procession—animals, people, houses—pass through the gate. The *almodo* gateway is also constructed after a lunar eclipse, to protect the village from misfortune.

The other important ritual blessing of camels is *sorio*, which is held four times a year (during two *sorio* months, followed four months later by another pair of months), on the eighth day of the specific *sorio* month. During *sorio*, all camels are brought back to the village and penned in their enclosures. Each house presents a small stock for sacrifice, which are killed in succession as all the settlement's men (and male children) move from house to house (women and girls are prohibited from viewing the events and sit inside the house). Outside in front of the door, several men hold the goat while the house's male elder "washes" the goat or sheep with milk, presenting it by hand to the animal's mouth, back, tail, and belly. The assembled men move their camel sticks over the goat's back, saying "*Sorio!*" As two men hold the animal in place, the elder cuts its throat, allowing the blood to collect in a small hole dug in the sand. All assembled men and boys dip the end of their camel sticks into the blood, and mark a little blood on their foreheads. Small boys then dip a handful of sisal fiber into the blood and mark the penned camels with a quick line of red on their right sides, below their humps. Women then cook the sacrificed animal, which is consumed by all members of the household.

Unlike *almodo*, which is a communitywide ritual, the *sorio* sacrifice is a personal offering asking for God's protection of one's own household. *Sorio* is not so austere that people don't joke a bit about as the men move from house to house to sacrifice each goat, similar to an American family's conversation while the Thanksgiving turkey is being carved. Moreover, *sorio* provides meat to the household at least four times a year, and is looked at with pleasure by Ariaal.

SORCERY AND THE ROLE OF THE *LAIBON*

While Ariaal do not have beliefs in ancestors or even defined deities, they do believe in sorcery and the power of *laibons* (diviner/medicine men) to inflict and protect against sorcery attacks. *Laibons* are male diviner-healers and ritual specialists found among Maa-speaking peoples of East Africa including Maasai, Samburu, LChamus, and Parakuyo pastoralists of Kenya and Tanzania. The Rendille and other Cushitic people do not have *laibons*, but sometimes consult a Samburu or Ariaal *laibon* if they are having problems. Born with an inherited ability to prophesy during dreams or intoxicated states, *laibons* (from the Maa verb *a-ibon*, to predict) also practice divination with "stones" thrown from a gourd or cow's horn. Furthermore, they have the ability to make mystically powerful medicines called *ntasim* used to protect against physical and supernatural attacks of sorcery, which are believed to be brought about by the jealousy of kin and neighbors. In the nineteenth century, contending *laibons* were powerful leaders among different Maasai groups, providing spiritual and political leadership during times of warfare, drought, and political upheavals. The Maasai people hold that the defeat of the Laikipiak Maasai by the Purko Maasai in the 1870s was due to the more powerful medicines of the Purko's *laibon* Mbatiany than those of the Laikipiak *laibon*. *Laibons* still have a special relationship with the warrior age-sets: the *laibon* provided protective medicines for both the warrior's age-grade ceremonies and for their military raids against enemies.

Beliefs in sorcery are widespread among the Ariaal. If a peculiar or strange misfortune befalls somebody, such as their animals get sick but no one else's do, or a woman has several miscarriages, or a person dies by lightening, drowning, or a lion attack, then sorcery is suspected. If a person believes he is ensorcelled, he must consult a *laibon*.

Sorcery is believed to be caused by mystically poisonous substances prepared in secret by *laibons*, often as a powder

The Laibon Leaduma and son Kanikis read divination stones, with Lugi Lengesen and Irionai Leriare.

made from certain roots and the burnt remains of snakes or chameleons. The sorcery poison may be placed on a stick that is thrown in one's cattle enclosure, or sprinkled near the doorway of a house. In times of warfare, sorcery poisons may be given to warriors by the *laibon* to place on a path enemies will cross, or mixed in the soil where enemy footprints are located.

The presence of sorcery is determined by a *laibon's* divination, often a private ritual conducted inside the house of the victim or that of the *laibon*. The divination ritual is a dialogue between the *laibon*, his clients, and the "stones," whose aim is to locate whether sorcery has been committed. Once a sorcery act is revealed, only a *laibon* can protect a sorcery victim with powerful *ntasim* medicines, worn as amulets tied to one's necklaces or marked on the forehead. Lugi, who believed in Leaduma's powers, told me, "If a person is cursed by sorcery (*nkurporen*), no hospital can cure that person. Only a laibon can help you." Because sorcery poisons are acquired from unscrupulous *laibons*, the *laibon's* curing ritual of divination and *ntasim* medicine is a the battle between *laibons* who know each other's identity, but seldom revealed to the larger public. The death of a *laibon* is almost always attributed to the sorcery of a rival *laibon*, as was that of my adopted father Lekati Leaduma who died at the age of 62.

As Leaduma's son, I witnessed several dozen of his curative rituals. I was struck by the degree to which sorcery accusations increased among the more isolated Ariaal communities, particularly those deep in the Ndoto Mountains distant from towns, hospitals, and police protection. The desire for the *laibon's* protective medicines appeared to be a direct consequence of isolation and anxiety about very real dangers of pastoral existence such as drought, cattle diseases, or danger from wild animals.

While I do not personally believe in the power of sorcery or divination, certain instances did occur that startled me during my fieldwork. Once in the middle of the night, I caught an old *lais* (Rendille with a strong curse) rummaging through my tin boxes while I slept. I awoke and asked him what he wanted, he replied, "Give me tobacco!" This man was a particularly irritating neighbor who was always begging tobacco from me. Annoyed, I shouted at him "If you want something, then ask for it, don't take it!" He shouted back, "Give me tobacco!" and I, perhaps irresponsibly, spoke to him as an adult speaks to a child "*Mutum!*, you can't have any!"

"What?" he replied to me, glaring with his eyebrows raised high. "You say '*Mutum*' to me? You will not see the sunset tomorrow! You will see fire!"

Well, I knew enough to know that I had been cursed, and cursed by a pretty powerful guy. So the next day I went over to Leaduma's house and said "Hey, last night the old *lais* cursed me for not giving him tobacco. What should I do?" Leaduma sighed and said "Don't worry about that old man. He cannot curse you because you wouldn't give him tobacco, and if he does, he will have to contend with me."

That seemed to settle the matter and I forgot about it until a few months later. Resting in my house during mid-day, I heard the terrible wailing of women coming from a large boulder about 500 yards from the village. This rock, about 50 feet high, had a long depression in it that trapped rain water, and the young women from the village had been going there for water after some heavy rains. I ran there with the others, where I saw on the rock above four or five warriors waist deep in the pool of water, reaching down in search of something. Oh lord, someone had drowned, and these men, who do not know how to swim, were trying to get the person out. I jumped into the pool and felt a deep and narrow crevice at one end, where the person had obviously fallen and got trapped. I asked the warriors to push me by my ankles into the crevice, and to be sure to pull me out again. Inside the narrow crevice, I felt a child's foot, and pulled a young girl out. Although I tried resuscitating her, I was unsuccessful and the young girl, about ten years old, was dead. People were moved that I tried to save her, but they were horrified that I put my mouth on hers, for they feared that I had swallowed her "death" and would also die. That evening, I was given a large number of herbal medicines that made me retch violently, to expurgate the darkness of the day's events. As I was recovering, however,

Leaduma softly spoke to me. "That girl, she was the daughter of the *Lais*. He had been cursed by many people, and this is what comes of that." His words did not comfort me, but only made me sadder. Why did an innocent child have to pay the price of her father's activities?

In this difficult land, where misfortune, accident, and hardship are a constant threat, beliefs in sorcery are strongly held, and the *laibon's* medicines of protection are sought after by most people.

WOMEN'S RITES OF PASSAGE

Ariaal women, while not formally conscripted in age-sets, nevertheless pass through distinct periods as preadolescents, adolescents, married women, mothers, and, for many, as single widowed women in their later life. At the onset of puberty, or a few years earlier, girls will begin to wear more elaborate neck beads and red line makeup on their faces, and begin to socialize with circumcised warriors. Most girls are "beaded" by warriors, that is, made steady girlfriends (and sexual partners) by young men of their clan who present a large quantity of beads, often over one hundred dollars worth, which the girls fashion into head bands, necklaces, and leather skirts for themselves, or into bracelets, armlets, and necklaces for their boyfriends. While spending time with warriors, a girl will avoid married elders, even leaving her mother's house if her father enters.

These romantic relationships form the basis of much of the music, poetry, and songs of the warriors and their girlfriends, but they are often short lived. The girl's father and uncles arrange her marriage when she is between 16 and 20 years old, usually to a man at least one age-set senior to that of her warrior lover. Male dominance over women is virtually assured by the large age difference between spouses at marriage, where men are in their thirties and women in their late teens. If the male is taking a second or third wife, a young women may marry a man in his sixties or older.

A woman seldom chooses her husband and is not party to the marriage negotiations. Her prospective spouse (who she may or may not know) declares his marriage intentions to the girl's father and his kin, using an intermediary (usually the groom's father's brother) to make the initial approach. If the girl's family agrees to the union, negotiations over bride price are made. Ideally this should include eight cattle, one of which is killed and eaten during the wedding ceremony. However, most marriage payments are a combination of small stock (goats and sheep), large stock, and occasionally cash, paid out over a long period and even into the next generation. Marriage negotiations are a male-to-male enterprise, and the economics of bride price seals the two families, and especially the men, into a lifelong alliance and source of assistance and aid.

On the wedding day the groom and his best man arrive at the bride's village to present the wedding ox to the bride's father, having carefully guarded the ox on the previous night to prevent elopement (if a suitor kills the wedding ox before the groom does, he may "take" the bride as his own). The groom and his clansmen ritually kill the ox (by suffocating the animal and inserting a knife through the base of its skull), providing the meat for the wedding feast. The meat is

Killing the wedding ox

divided by the bride's father, who distributes it based on set rules of relationships, such as the right front leg to the father, brother, and so on.

While the ox is being killed, the bride is undergoing "female circumcision" (clitoridectomy), an operation in which a local midwife cuts and removes the clitoris and part (or all) of the labia minora. (Ariaal do not practice infibulation, the suturing of the labia, which occurs in some parts of northeastern Africa.) Showing extraordinary fortitude, the bride will come out of the house in a few hours to greet the guests at the wedding who have been feasting on the wedding ox. At one wedding, I could hear the young bride arguing inside the wedding house, "I don't want to do this, I don't even know this man, please don't make me do this." But the older women told her to be strong, that they had to go through this, and that it would be over soon.

Ariaal women showed surprise and disdain when I told them we do not circumcise women in my country. The wife of one elder told me in consciously contradictory terms:

It is bad that you don't circumcise women in your country. That child which is born to such a woman, is it human? We think it is bad to bear a child if the woman is not circumcised. But you know, the men like to see us circumcised. They think we won't see other men if we are circumcised. But they are wrong [she laughed].

Matrescence, the bearing and raising of children, is considered the most important role in a woman's life, and women with many children are admired by all. Conversely, "barren" women or those with only a few children are not only pitied but feared, as it is thought they may do harm to other children out of jealousy. Infertility (which is high, due mainly to sexually transmitted diseases, especially gonorrhea and chlamydia) is considered a spiritual misfortune, brought about by bad fate or human enemies using sorcery to harm someone. Women go to great length to protect themselves when pregnant, and particularly don't like strangers (or tourists with cameras) looking directly at them lest they harm the infant with an "evil eye." Because both infertility and infant mortality is high, there are many prohibitions associated with birth including eating the right foods, avoiding sex when pregnant or nursing, and not exposing the mother and infant to undue risk and hardship. Given the high number of infant and child deaths (two out of five children do not reach their sixth year), women need to produce many children in the hope that one son will survive to take care of her in her old age.

A widow may not remarry in Ariaal, nor is she permitted to divorce or return to her natal home, as her family is reluctant to return a bride price that has been used to help her brothers marry. There is a large number of widows in every Ariaal settlement, mainly because women, much younger than the men they marry, often outlive their husbands. Young widows who are still reproductive continue to bear children fathered by her husband's kin. These children are considered legitimate heirs of their fathers, although they grow up socially stigmatized.

THE STATUS OF WOMEN

Anthropologists have long had an interest in the comparative study of women in different societies, but the field is still full of debate. Some anthropologists as well as human rights activists, both in the west and in the developing world, argue that women are treated unequally to men in terms of access to resources (including food, employment, and wealth), power to make decisions governing their own and their children's lives, and control over their individual destinies. On the other side of the debate are cultural representatives and their supporters (including some anthropologists) who argue that standards of women's status are relative and cannot be judged solely from a western viewpoint, and that women in traditional societies gain much prestige and satisfaction from cultural values emphasizing motherhood, fertility, and their contributions to household life.

Anthropologists who study pastoralist women in Africa have pointed to women's unequal status based on lack of ownership rights in livestock; lack of decision-making ability in marriage, divorce, and control over children; and lack of political voice in village and extra-village affairs. This pattern of inequality is evident among the Ariaal. While Ariaal women gain prestige and status through the successes of their husband and children, in my opinion they are disempowered, as men own all property and control women's labor. Although Ariaal women receive a herd of milk stock from their husbands at marriage and have defined rights to certain animals, they do not own these animals. Rather, they are used to feed the household, and the women cannot sell or give away these animals, nor can they build up herds of their own. While a widow can exercise some control over her deceased husband's herd, particularly when her children are small, this is only in trust until her male children are old enough to marry. Furthermore, as my time allocation surveys show, women work hard in activities associated with livestock production, but they do not receive the rewards of this labor in the same way men do. Unlike younger brothers or hired herders who receive some payment for herding labor, women receive none, either in cash or livestock. The inequality in property ownership is evident.

Dependent on their fathers as children, and on their husbands as adults, women enter old age (and typically widowhood) dependent on their sons to feed and care for them. Men, on the other hand, are assured that the public and jural (legal) spheres are their exclusive domains, by virtue of their control of livestock capital.

However, it should also be noted that women have a say in household affairs such as decisions to relocate or send a child to school. There are many married couples among Ariaal who have meaningful and mutually supportive relationships. There are also marriages characterized by domestic violence against women, although these are usually kept hidden from public view.

A women's ability to produce children and thus expand the household labor force strikes me as a leading reason Ariaal uphold polygyny (multiple marriage by men) as a

The widow Lengesen scrapes a cow hide.

cultural ideal. Although polygyny may not affect the fertility rate (some studies suggest polygyny may actually decrease the number of children a woman has), male elders can obtain more labor—both from women and their future children—through multiple marriages. The polygyny rate in Lewogoso in 1985 was 1.39, where almost one-half of the married men had more than one wife. A few wealthier men have three wives each. Both women and men informants in Ariaal value polygyny because of its contribution to the labor supply. Men state that multiple wives produce more children to herd animals, and women prefer having a cowife with whom they can share household tasks. "I begged my husband to find another wife," said one Lewogoso woman, "so I don't have to fetch water, collect firewood, and milk the animals all by myself." Melissa Llewelyn-Davies, who made the film *Masai Women*, shows how Maasai women, who arrive as strangers to their husband's home village, form tight bonds of solidarity with other women and particularly co-wives.

Ariaal women endure male domination in both ideology and control of economic resources. There are always exceptions of course. One is a woman I call *"Paker"* (meaning mother-in-law, or "receiver of the wedding sheep"), because I used to tease her eight-year-old daughter that I would marry her one day. Paker was a wealthy widow whose husband died when she was young, and who managed her substantial household herds until her children had grown. Although she did not own these animals in a strict sense, she engaged in many husbandry decisions (deciding which animals to breed) and managed the sales of her livestock. Maintaining a reputation as a shrewd and responsible stock keeper, this woman often participated in discussions with Lewogoso elders over grazing decisions, where and when to move the settlement, and political questions relating to the larger government. This was done privately, however, and not in the usual context of men's discussions in their shade area or in the men's ritual center, the *naabo*. However, in time, as her sons married, Paker's status diminished and she became another of the settlement's "old women" (*ntasat*), lacking prestige, power, and basic security.

In another household lived Ndepeyan, a young widow with a small son and daughter, who owned 20 cattle and 26 small stock. Although her late husband's brothers tried to take away her animals, Ndepeyan refused. She herded her small stock with another kinsman's animals, and hired a male youth from a neighboring household to herd her cattle. In 1995, Ndepeyan moved to Ngurunit town to escape the demands of her husband's brothers, and continues to manage her animals until her son marries. Ndepeyan is one of a few women who stand out as independent women who manages her own animals and refuses to submit to her husband's family. For the majority of women, however, few had the means to support an independent life free of the control of their fathers, husbands, and sons. This situation changes dramatically, however, when Ariaal and Rendille move to agricultural communities, as the discussion of Songa village in Chapter 6 shows.

SUMMARY

The Ariaal are the product of a long-standing alliance between Samburu and Rendille society, and they have formed a unique bridge culture combining elements of the two larger traditions. They follow Samburu rituals centered around cattle production, including the *mugit* ox feasts marking stages in their age-set system, but they also follow Rendille rites associated with the well being of their camels, particularly the *almodo* blessings and *sorio* sacrifices. Integrated into the Samburu clans, they also share Samburu and Maasai beliefs in sorcery and the power of *laibons.*

Ariaal identity is ambiguous. Ariaal are not considered wholly Samburu, as many come from Rendille families, raise camels as well as cattle and small stock, live in large desert settlements, follow Rendille ceremonies blessing camels, and recite evening prayers in the village's ritual center (the *naabo*). But Rendille see Ariaal as more Samburu than Rendille because of their cattle-raising, their inclusion in the Samburu segmentary descent system, and their following Samburu forms of birth, marriage, death, and age-set rituals.

Tribal identity is as ambiguous to Ariaal as it is to outsiders. Kitoip Lenkiribe, who had spoken earlier about the shifta raids, remarked:

> We're really something in between Samburu and Rendille. We are not something different, we are really both things together. We live in Rendille country, keep camels, and follow [camel-blessing rites] *sorio* and *almodo*. Although we stay away from the *gaalgulamme* [Rendille age-set initiation ritual] as we do not think the Rendille want us there, we do send our camels there to be blessed. Our houses are Rendille, and we speak both languages. Yet we also keep cattle, we follow the Samburu *mugit* [age-set rites], and speak in Samburu language. If I was in Nairobi and someone asked me who I was, I would say Samburu. But when I'm in Maralal [the capital of Samburu District], they call me "filthy Rendille,"

and when I'm in Korr [a Rendille center], they call me Ariaal. But in fact, Lewogoso [an Ariaal and Samburu subclan] and Tubsha [a Rendille clan] are brothers—we came from the same people a long time ago. The younger brothers of Rendille families [i.e., those without camel inheritances] came toward Samburu, or Samburu came down into the lowlands to keep camels; they are now the same people who live in the same country.

Ariaal society is unique and distinct from Rendille and Samburu. While they have borrowed customs from both societies, the fact is that Ariaal consciously mix and fuse these elements. Furthermore Ariaal recognize themselves as a distinct group, with their own local clans, territory, and way of life. They are, in fact, a distinct social formation.

4

A Pastoral Life: Livestock Production and Human Nutrition

The Ariaal live in a semi-desert environment of very sparse resources. Low and variable rainfall, marked seasonality in vegetation growth, and few watering areas make the Marsabit District too dry to support agriculture on a wide scale, and nearly all the area's residents depend on domestic livestock to survive. From the perspective of human ecology, pastoralists use their domestic animals to convert patchy and seasonal vegetative resources into a constant supply of food in the form of milk, meat, blood, and a surplus with which to trade for grains, tea, and sugar.

The semi-desert of northern Kenya supports a variety of animals, both domestic and wild, despite its aridity. Grazing side by side with Ariaal cattle, camels, goats, and sheep are reticulated giraffe, Grant's gazelles, gerenuks (desert antelopes with long necks), and elephants, as well as lions, cheetahs, leopards, hyenas, and wild dogs who prey on these herbivores. These animals can be seen at the Samburu Game Park, one of Kenya's most beautiful, which is located on the Uaso Nyriu River in Eastern Samburu District just south of my study area in the Ndoto Mountains.

The essential strategy of livestock pastoralism is to ensure adequate grazing and water for livestock to provide a regular food supply for the human community. Herders follow various strategies aimed at keeping their herds productive through both rainy and dry seasons, as well as deal with periodic and extensive drought. The two most important strategies for the Ariaal are species diversity and herding mobility.

Species diversity, keeping different types of livestock rather than specializing in one type of animal, enables a pastoralist to utilize different grazing environments as well as provide insurance against particular herd losses caused by diseases such as bovine pneumonia for cattle or trypanosomiasis in camels. During extensive droughts in 1984, 1992, and 1996, when Samburu and Ariaal lost over half their cattle, Ariaal were able to rely on their camels, which were relatively unscathed. Furthermore, the keeping of different types of animals offers complementary food resources as well as different breeding and milking cycles. Ariaal rely on their camels for milk and transport, their small stock of goats and sheep for meat and trade, and their cattle to provide both traditional exchange values (including eight cattle necessary to marry and oxen to sacrifice at the *mugit* age-set rituals) and trade in the commercial market for cash.

Mobility is of equal, if not greater, importance than herd diversity to the pastoralist. Because of the high seasonality in rainfall and the high evaporation rate, vegetation resources deteriorate very quickly. Herds are taken to new green pastures following isolated rainfall, as pastures are more nutritive during growing season, with higher proportions of crude protein and carbohydrates. These movements are limited mainly by the availability of drinking water, which, although widespread in the wet seasons, is found only in a few areas with permanent water holes during the dry season. The responsibility of feeding their animals is perhaps the single greatest factor affecting Ariaal settlement and labor organization.

Each type of stock has its own particular feeding and water requirements. Cattle are grazers (grass eaters) who need water every two to three days, and consequently must be herded in the wetter highlands. Camels are adapted to desert conditions, preferring browse (leaves) of shrubs and trees that thrive when grasses dry out. Furthermore, camels can go without watering for ten days, offering enough time for their herders to graze them extensively in the desert lowlands between fixed water points. Small stock can thrive in the deserts, but like cattle need water every two to three days, and must be grazed near the mountain springs and wells.

Because of these different herding requirements, Ariaal separate their animals into different herds, keeping milk and male transport camels as well as small stock in the domestic settlements, while herding non-milking cattle in highland grazing areas for long periods of time. Ariaal are not long distance nomads. Their settlements are semi-sedentary, located near permanent water sources and small urban centers along the Ndoto Mountains or Mt. Marsabit. People do not generally live closer than ten kilometers to the water holes, as they fear overgrazing the available vegetation and choose to graze their animals at greater distances. The chance of finding better pastures increases with the distance from the water points, and settlements with large numbers of transport camels will live farthest from towns or water sources.

RAINFALL AND WATER RESOURCES

Marsabit District is the most arid region in Kenya, receiving an average of 500 mm (less than ten inches) of rainfall each year. In the lowlands, temperatures average 27.8°C (82°F), but often reach over 38°C (100°F) midday, while the highlands can be chilly, averaging 18.9°C (66.0°F). Rainfall on Mt. Marsabit and Mt. Kulal may exceed 1000 mm (40 inches) annually, but may be less than 200 mm (8 inches) a year in the Kaisut and Chalbi Deserts, if it rains at all. Rainfall is erratic and irregular in quantity and timing, and no one can predict where, when, or how much rain will fall. Drought has occurred every four or five years since 1968, in marked contrast to the first half of the century which saw above average rainfalls.

Rainfall is concentrated in two short seasons, a long rain (*lng'erng'erwa*) between March and May, and a short rain (*ltumerin*) in October and November. The period between November and March is called "the long hunger" (*lamai lo'odo*), and between June and October the "short hunger" (*lamai dorrop*). This rainfall pattern is determined largely by changing seasonal winds around the equator, alternatively bringing dry high-pressure air from Arabia in the winter (the northeast trade winds), and moist low-pressure air (the southeast trade winds) from the Indian Ocean in the summer.

Rainfall is critical for two reasons: it directly determines vegetation growth and the availability of pasture for the livestock; and it provides drinking water for the human and livestock populations. During rainy seasons, Ariaal have sufficient use of surface water in rain pools, semi-permanent rivers, and temporary flood plains, the most important surface water being the river runoffs from the Ndoto and Mathew's Range Mountains along the Ngurunit, Milgis, Merille, and Uaso Nyiru rivers. These rivers are sand-bedded, and the water quickly flows underground as it descends off the mountain. The Milgis River becomes a seasonal swamp west of Baiyo Mountain (called Larapasie), and is an important wet season watering point for Ariaal cattle and small stock. It is also the home of the Lewogoso Lukumai settlement.

During the long dry seasons, Ariaal must obtain water from hand-dug wells, often chiseled out of rock, located at points in the river beds where underground rock traps the laterally flowing water. Saline water, found at the wells at Korr, Koroli, and Halisuruwa, is much preferred by camels, while cattle like the "sweet" water of the highlands. The locations of these water sources have been known to pastoralists through generations of trial and error digging, and searches for new water sources using modern techniques by government and development agencies have led to no new water sources. Increasingly communities have adopted suggestions and aid from various NGOs such as Food for the

Hungry to build concrete water catchments off rock outcroppings and dig new wells.

VEGETATION

Arid lands are rarely barren, but have their own interesting vegetation, generally distinguished by different altitudes that receive differing amounts of rainfall. Vegetation in Marsabit District falls within four ecological zones:

- Highland forests above 2000 meters consisting of evergreen forests constituting 5% of the Ariaal grazing area.
- Savanna-woodlands at 1000 to 1400 meters characterized by *Acacia* trees ("umbrella" or thorn trees) and with a dense grass cover. This ecological zone, located mainly in the highlands of Mt. Marsabit and the Ndotos Mountains, makes up less than 10% of the Ariaal herding environment but is the area most important used by Ariaal cattle for grazing and water.
- Arid scrub bush between 700 and 1000 meters, representing about 30% of Ariaal resources. This semi-desert of mixed *acacia-commiphora* trees and perennial grasses offers the main dry season grazing for Ariaal camels and location for Ariaal settlements.
- Very arid lowland desert comprising 55% of the Ariaal area (the Kaisut Desert) at an altitude of 200 to 800 meters and receiving annual rainfall less than 200 mm (8 inches). Despite its extreme aridity, periodic rains will produce a large but short-lived growth of annual grasses and shrubs which are eaten by camels and small stock in the short wet seasons.

Ariaal also utilize two micro-environments in the area: lava plateaus (called *marti*) found throughout the arid semi-desert, providing shrubs and grasses eaten by camels and small stock, and river beds. Ariaal settlements are often located close to these river beds, providing shade, wood for fences, containers, and spear shafts, and seeds which are eaten by small stock.

ARIAAL LIVESTOCK

Ariaal own large numbers of livestock, with an average household of 5 people keeping 12 camels, 20 cattle, and 50 small stock. These numbers are similar to the Rendille, but Ariaal have larger cattle herds and smaller camel holdings. Ariaal cattle herds are smaller than Samburu or Maasai, where herds can reach several hundred per household. However, Ariaal rely more on their mixture of livestock types (cattle, camels, and small stock), and utilize a greater variety of habitat than Samburu or Rendille.

Despite the large sizes of Ariaal herds, these animals are highly variable in productivity, both in milk and meat off take and in the growth rates of the herds. In general, Ariaal animals reproduce in low numbers and suffer high mortality due to high rates of disease, infection, malnutrition, and parasite loads, particularly during and immediately after extensive droughts. Ariaal lose cattle to drought, primarily by starvation or pneumonia, while their camels, suffering less from drought, lose thirty percent of their immature stock to trypanosomiasis (from tsetse flies), tick-borne toxins, respiratory illnesses, and other infectious diseases. Prolonged rains create conditions for pneumonia among goats and sheep, as well as weaken their hooves and ability to feed. The heavy rains during the 1997 El Niño killed 75% of Ariaal small stock from disease and starvation.

The Ariaal strategy for coping with these hazards is to keep large numbers of different food-producing stock (cattle, camels, goats, and sheep), maximize their herd sizes as insurance against catastrophic loss, and disperse their animals by herding their livestock in separate areas and loaning their animals to friends and kin in distant areas.

Ariaal depend on their livestock primarily for milk for seventy percent of the diet in the pastoral settlements. This is complemented by meat, store-bought grains, sugar, and tea, and occasionally blood tapped from living animals. Ariaal herds, like those of other African subsistence pastoralists, are mainly female (estimated at 55% of the cattle, 60%–70% of the camels, and 50–60% of their small stock) with a high proportion of mature adults so that fifteen to 25% of their livestock are producing milk at any given time. Males are kept primarily for meat, exchange, and in the case of camels and donkeys, used for transport. All male animals are castrated, save one or two kept as breeding bulls and rams.

CAMELS

Camels are the Ariaal's most reliable food source, yielding an average of 3.5 liters of milk daily and reaching 10 liters daily in wet seasons. Humans share the milk in roughly equal amounts with nursing calves. In general, humans can depend on 2.0 liters of milk from each lactating camel daily. The supply of camel milk is lengthy and copious, as lactation lasts from 9–18 months and does not end during the dry season as it may with cattle or small stock.

Camels are remarkable animals with an ability to thrive in deserts areas characterized by high temperatures, lack of water, and plant life too saline for other ruminants. They can go without watering almost two weeks, and are watered by Ariaal every ten days, allowing them to be grazed over a wide area. The adaptations of camels to arid regions are based on their ability to utilize available moisture and their economical expenditure of body fluids, including very dry feces and highly concentrated urine.

Despite (or because of) their adaptation to arid lands, camels have a very low growth rate of 1.5 percent annually due to a low number of births and high mortality, particularly of nursing calves. A camel dam drops her first calf in her sixth year, following a long gestation period of 12–13 months. A long lactation period averaging 12 months contributes to a 20–30 month birth interval. An estimated 30–60% of Ariaal calves die, primarily because of trypanosomes (blood parasites) and toxins produced by heavy tick infestations. The avoidance of these insects is a major reason Ariaal settlements are located away from mountain locations, with their greater density of vegetation and arthropod vectors of disease. Other diseases found in camel populations include viral infections (rinderpest, foot and mouth disease, rabies), bacteria (tuberculosis, salmonellosis, contagious pleuropneumonia, glanders), large internal parasites (intestinal worms, coccidiosis, leishmaniasis, arterial filariasis), and external parasites (mange, ticks). Studies by veterinary scientists in the area show that adequate veterinary care could improve camel productivity by 100%, particularly if worm loads were reduced.

In addition to milk production, camels are the main pack animal of both Ariaal and Rendille proper. Male animals transport houses and household goods during settlement relocations, and fetch water for human consumption. Women and girls are responsible for loading and working the transport camels, and will collect water for the household every third or fourth day, labor that usually requires a walk of ten to fifteen kilometers.

Ariaal warrior herding cattle.

CATTLE

Ariaal keep the Borana breed of East African Zebu cattle, drought-resistant livestock who entered Africa from the Mideast in the past 300 years. These animals are character- ized by a back hump (which, like the camel, stores fat and provides calories in drought conditions), short horns, and a loose skin fold (dewlap) under the neck, which helps the an- imal cool. Borana cattle have a hardy reputation for surviv- ing in dry and marginal rangeland, eating grasses when possible, but subsisting on browse if necessary.

Despite their hardiness, Ariaal cattle cannot survive in the dry lowlands to which camels are so well suited, be- cause of the cattle's need to drink water at least once every three days (and preferably every other day). Because of their need for salt, which is found in natural salt licks along high- land river beds, and the need for grass which grows in greater quantity in the humid highlands, cattle are herded primarily in the highlands. Fortunately, cattle can tolerate higher tick loads—which are more abundant in the forested highlands—than camels.

Cattle produce much less milk than camels, yielding slightly more than 1.0 liter in wet periods and a quarter of that in the dry season. One camel in year-round lactation can support as many people as four cows. Cattle lactate for a period of 3–8 months annually (with about 60% of the herd being female and fifty percent lactating per year) and can provide between 0.5 and 1.5 liters of milk for human con- sumption daily. Table 4.1 shows East African livestock pro- duction characteristics.

Although their milk production is low, cattle have a high reproductive rate, twice that of camels, with 9 months gesta- tion, 8 months lactation, and a year-round mating period. A cow can be expected to reproduce after 17 months; a camel has a birth interval of over 26 months.

This high birth rate produces a surplus of cattle that con- tributes to their use for trade and rituals. Eight cattle consti- tute Ariaal bride price, and steers are ritually slaughtered at weddings and age-set ceremonies. A main economic role for cattle in Ariaal is as a traditional exchange medium for

TABLE 4.1 PRODUCTION CHARACTERISTICS OF EAST AFRICAN LIVESTOCK

	Camels	Cattle	Goats	Sheep
Mean weight	300 kg	164.7	24.8	23.7
Daily milk yields for human consumption, liters				
Wet season	2.5	1.3	0.23	0.22
Dry season	1.2	0.5	0.09	0.07
Lactation length (mo.)	12	6.9	4.6	4.5
Herd growth rate (%)	1.5	2.5	11	11
Birthing interval (mo.)	24	18	5.5	8.3

Source: Dahl and Hjort (1976); IPAL (1984); and N. Dyson-Hudson and R. Dyson-Hudson (1982).

wives, and Ariaal men will try to build up their cattle herds to gain additional wives in polygyny. Cattle are also increasingly becoming the main source of cash income for Ariaal, providing more than half of their cash needs through trade and livestock auctions.

Ariaal stock owners prefer to sell cattle rather than camels because of their high growth rate, the relatively high prices cattle fetch on the market, and their lower milk yields. The role of cattle as a cash provider is particularly important to Ariaal who depend on store-bought maizemeal to supplement or substitute for milk during the dry seasons. In 1985, the average Lewogoso household spent 1200 shillings ($75.00). Grain purchases were substantially higher in the settled towns like Korr where Ariaal and Rendille families, largely without stock, were buying maizemeal (posho) daily, spending over 1500 shillings a year and receiving from the mission free *posho* and powdered milk during drought or other hardship conditions.

SMALL STOCK

"Small stock (goats and sheep) are our bank," Lugi once told me, as they can be sold readily or given as gifts when relatives and important visitors show up. Ariaal keep large numbers of small stock, ranging from 40 to 300 goats and sheep per household. Small stock are an important part of Ariaal pastoral economy because of their high reproductive rate, their ability to survive in arid conditions, their easy convertibility to cash, and because they provide a ready source of meat.

Ariaal keep goats of the Small East African type and sheep of the short-haired Somali (Persian) breed which weigh about 20 kilograms each. More goats are kept than sheep (a ratio of 2:1), a fact attributed to the better adaptability of goats to arid environments. Sheep and goats are herded together and called by a collective name (*ntare* for mixed flocks; *lkine* (*lkineji* pl.) for goats and *nker* (*nkerra* pl.) for sheep). Like camels, small stock prefer to graze in the hot tickless plains where goats eat browse (twigs and leaves) and sheep prefer grasses. Their high water needs, however, demand that small stock are grazed near permanent water sources, usually close to the mountain foothills. For much of the year, small stock remain with the domestic settlements; only in very dry situations are they grazed in camps. Small stock are difficult to herd because individuals wander off, and because they easily develop infections from thorns or stones between the hooves, particularly in wet conditions.

Goats and sheep are poor milk producers. During a three-month lactation period a goat can be expected to provide 200 cc of milk daily in wet periods, and as little as 50 cc in the dry periods; hence 20 goats are necessary to provide 1 liter of milk in the dry months. Their primary importance lies in their high reproductive rates due to a short birth interval, short gestation period, and a high number of twin births. Ariaal rely on building up their small stock following a drought, for they recover quickly and can be traded for cash or directly for large livestock, particularly cattle.

Small stock are important mainly for their meat. They are killed with increasing frequency as the dry season progresses, and it is not unusual for a household to butcher a goat or sheep each week. In addition to consuming the meat, hides are made into women's skirts or sold to traders for small amounts (150 Kenyan shillings or US $2). Small stock also are a ready source of cash, as they can be readily sold for prices ranging from 1000 Kenya shillings (US $14) to 2000 Kenya shillings (US $28), contributing up to forty percent of a household's cash needs.

MISCELLANEOUS ANIMALS

Ariaal also keep donkeys and dogs, neither of which are used for food. Donkeys are kept as pack animals by some Ariaal, particularly those in the highlands owing to the donkey's high water and grazing needs. They are not found widely among lowland Ariaal who use male camels for transporting water and household goods.

Ariaal keep dogs to warn against predators (over half of Lewogoso households had at least one dog). These animals are small (ten to fifteen kilograms), short-haired, red-and-white or black-and-white basenji-type animals (although unlike basenjis, they bark). I found these dogs singularly hostile and unattractive, all skin and bones, full of worms, and covered with ticks and camel flies. Ariaal confess that their dogs are treated worse than any other type of livestock they own, but keep them to bark warnings of predators.

THE DIVISION OF CAMP AND SETTLEMENT

Ariaal separate their livestock into "domestic" herds—those necessary for the maintenance of the settlement including milk and transport animals, and "camp" stock, adolescent, male, and non-milking female animals which are grazed in more mobile herding camps, often for long periods of time. These camps (called *fora* in Rendille and *lalei* in Samburu) are managed by warriors and allow the Ariaal to maximize pasture availability by taking their cattle up to the highlands and camels deep into the desert lowlands. Domestic herds are grazed near the settlement, returning each night where they are protected by the village's thorn-bush enclosures. Adolescent boys are usually responsible for herding milk camels, while adolescent girls and younger boys watch over the small stock as they graze near the village. The watering of all livestock is usually supervised by married men or warriors.

During the dry season, which can last many months per year, warriors take the cattle to highland locations, returning home to the settlements only during brief rains when there is sufficient grazing in the lowlands. Life in the camps is austere and dangerous. Warriors make temporary enclosures by cutting long branches off thorny *acacia* trees to encircle the cattle when they sleep. The warriors sleep in the open on top of cow skins, covered with nothing more than their thin cotton cloths. While they may have an aluminum pot to cook tea and porridge, these foods are not always available and the warriors must content themselves with drinking milk, blood, and soups made from wild plants. Occasionally the warriors may slaughter a goat to roast, but this may not happen for several weeks at a time.

I lived in the highland camps for short periods, one to two weeks, which is nothing compared to warriors who spend months at a time in the highlands with their animals, but the experience gave me a glimpse of the social world of Ariaal warriors. It is in the herding camps that strong bonds of friendship between warriors are created and maintained. The evenings are filled with songs about raids they had gone on, the beauty of their girlfriends, and their fights with enemies or wild animals. Camp life is dangerous, injuries are not uncommon, and medical care is miles away. It is not unusual for predators to attack animals in the camps, either at night or during the day while grazing. While hyenas and leopards tend to go after small stock, lions pursue cattle and camels. Once I was asked to treat a camel that had been attacked by a lion. The animal was still on its feet, but it had four enormous holes in its neck, two on each side of the windpipe (lions often kill by strangulation). I squeezed antibiotic ointment into the wounds and watched it for several days to make sure the wounds were draining, and the camel (miraculously) lived. On another occasion, I actually helped chase a lion who had jumped over the thorn fence into the camp. The warriors leapt to their feet, grabbing their spears as well as my flashlight, and we chased it into the darkness. Fortunately, the lion ran off. I am certain I would not have been able to kill it, although I know of warriors, including my brother Kanikis, who have successfully killed a lion with one well placed spear throw. This time, the warriors set a trap by killing a goat and filling its chest cavity with poison prepared from the *morijoi* tree (*Acokanthera longiflora*). We could hear the sick lion moan and roar all night, until the warriors finally caught up with it and speared it to death. While Ariaal loathe predators that destroy their livestock, they have a strong respect for lions, singing a praise song when they have killed one, and wearing a strip of lion skin around their wrist.

While most of Lewogoso's cattle were herded in the mountains in the mobile camps, nearly all of the milking camels and their nursing calves, as well as male camels used for transport, remain in the settlement. Transport camels are important not only to help move the houses during migrations, but also to bring water necessary for the human community. Eric Roth and I noticed that those households with transport camels were able to live farther from wells and towns, and thus have more pasture to feed their domestic herds. It is usually the task of adolescent girls to fetch water from the wells using loading camels. It is no small feat getting a male camel to fold its legs and descend so you can tie loading saddles and water containers on it, a task usually done by married women. When fetching water from the wells, girls will lead groups of three to four camels, each loaded with four round water containers made of woven sisal around a clay core. Each container (called *l-pira*) holds about ten gallons, and can provide a household with enough water for cooking and some washing for two to three days. Each house has two to three containers, allowing a week's worth of water and avoiding the long trek to the wells (often fifteen kilometers, a three-hour walk each way). Ariaal are very conservative about water use, for obvious reasons. Milk containers, for example, are not washed with water, but cleaned by placing smoky burning embers inside, giving the milk, and tea flavored with it, a distinctively smoky taste.

Women loading water containers.

THE HERDING ROUTINE OF LEWOGOSO LUKUMAI SETTLEMENT

Like most East African pastoralists, Ariaal are local rather than long-distance herders, moving their animals in independent herding groups orbiting around semi-permanent locations, cattle to the highlands, camels deep into the desert lowlands, with most of the small stock and milk camels living with the settlements. Herders from the Lewogoso Lukumai clan claim the area along the Ndoto Mountains near Larapasie swamp and the Milgis River, although in drought periods they will take their animals as far south as the Uaso Nyiru river near Isiolo, and as far west as Baragoi and Mt. Nyiru in the Samburu District.

Lewogoso cattle spend very little time in the domestic settlement except during the rare times when rainfall and pasture are plentiful. For the most part, the cattle are grazed in the highland valleys of the Ndoto Mountains or taken northwest one hundred kilometers to the LBarta plains in Samburu District. But the Turkana also graze heavily in this area, and Ariaal will only go there when there are large numbers of Samburu and Rendille using the area.

Where cattle graze in distant camps in the highlands, Lewogoso's camels are herded closer to the settlement, often returning at night from grazing or watering. During extensive droughts, non-milking camels are taken to distant *fora* (herding camps) in the Rendille areas. Ariaal prefer to live with their camels, and will keep most camels in the settlement rather than send them to *fora*. Highland Ariaal such as those living in Karare village on Mt. Marsabit will keep large numbers of cattle, but for the most part do not keep small stock or camels due to the large numbers of ticks in the highlands.

Herding patterns respond not only to climatic variation, but also to political pressures. In 1992, a severe drought year, Gabra herders (who had been quite peaceful toward their neighbors) began a series of armed raids against Rendille, Dasenech, and Boran livestock herds, and many Ariaal were afraid of grazing their camels in the north. Rendille moved *en masse* to Korr town, and Ariaal took their animals far south toward Isiolo and the Uaso Nyiru River. By 1994, raids with the Gabra had ceased, and Lewogoso herded their cattle as usual in highland locations such as Irrer in the Ndotos Mountains, while keeping most of their small stock and camels within the domestic settlements located between Baiyo Mountain and Ngurunit town. However, during the drought of 1996, many Ariaal and Rendille took their animals to Samburu District but were attacked by Turkana who killed seventeen people and took 15,000 animals. Although they recovered most of their animals, Ariaal pulled back to the security of Marsabit District.

THE DIVISION OF LABOR IN PRODUCTION TASKS

Much of the Ariaal's daily labor is expended on tasks managing their animal herds. The care of livestock never stops, they require attention from sunrise to late evening including finding adequate grazing, water and salt, and human protection to survive. Even at night when the animals are put into their enclosures, hungry predators or human enemies may attack and herders must be vigilant.

Production tasks in Ariaal are performed by different social categories based on age and gender roles in the division of labor. Adolescent boys and warriors perform most of the camel and cattle herding tasks; adolescent girls and small boys herd the domestic small stock near the settlement, adolescent girls fetch water from the wells utilizing pack camels, and young girls assist in child-care and fetch firewood. Married women milk the domestic settlement's cattle and small stock, maintain houses, and provide child-care and veterinary care to nursing stock. Married men, or elders, are responsible for animal husbandry (selecting bulls), milking camels, tracking lost animals, providing veterinary care, digging and maintaining wells, and undertaking ritual and political leadership for the settlement.

Camels are herded exclusively by men and boys. Boys between six and eleven years watch over juvenile and infant camels grazing near the settlement. Older adolescents and a few members of the warrior age-set accompany non-milking adult camels to *fora* camps and watering locations. Young boys may begin to accompany animals to *fora* by the time they are eight or nine years old.

Cattle are herded for much of the year in mountain camps managed predominately by members of the warrior age set but also by adolescent boys and girls. Girls are principally responsible for managing the small stock flocks which are usually herded from the domestic settlements close to the permanent water sources. Although there is a sexual division of labor in livestock tasks, it is apparent that unmarried girls play a significant role in livestock production, particularly in daily herding tasks.

In 1985 I conducted time allocation surveys of pastoral division of labor among people living in Lewogoso settlement. Equipped with code sheets that listed the gender, age, and particular tasks individuals could be doing, I would make unannounced visits to houses and areas at randomly selected times and locations. After three weeks, I had accumulated over 4000 spot observations, which I later grouped based on age and gender. For example, I found that woman spent 36.7 percent of their day in household tasks and fourteen percent of their day with animals, mainly milking animals but also herding and caring for young animals. Married men spent only 7.2% in household (a category which included "eating"!), and 33% of their time in livestock tasks, mainly inspecting the animals as they left and returned each day from grazing. Most herding tasks are performed by adolescent boys and warriors, who spent the most time in livestock tasks (83% and 71% of their daytime, respectively), while adolescent girls also spent a considerable time in herding and livestock activities (44%).

I also looked at how much time each individual had in rest or leisure activities. I was surprised to find that most Ariaal spent a fair amount of time resting, doing most of their arduous work in early morning and early evening, while resting during the hot part of the day. Even herders would rest under shade trees during the hot time of day, just as their animals did. But there were large differences between the rest time afforded to men versus women. Male elders (i.e., married men) had the most leisure time—more than half their daylight hours (52.4%) were spent sitting, talking, sleeping, or playing the *ndotoi* board game, while women rested about one third (35%) of their time. Even when sitting, however, women were doing some tasks such as cooking, caring for small children, or manufacturing (i.e. making beaded jewelry or weaving household mats from sisal). After analyzing these results, my wife Marty exclaimed "You need an $18,000 grant from the National Geographic Society to learn that women work harder than men?!"

LIVESTOCK PRODUCTION AND HUMAN NUTRITION

Ariaal production of camels, cattle, and small stock provide three types of foods to the human population—milk, meat, and blood. Milk is consumed daily by all members of the society, either fresh following the morning and evening milking, or curdled ("the milk that sleeps" *nkule na oto*), which is consumed mainly by older males. Milk provides 75% of their daily calories and 90% of their protein in the wet season, and 60% of their calories in the dry season. As milk supplies diminish in the dry season, blood is added to the milk, and more small stock are butchered to provide meat. In addition, small stock and cattle are sold to purchase maize meal, tea, and sugar. Cash income from livestock and skin sales is also used to buy cloth, rubber sandals, cooking utensils, and beads for jewelry.

Camels are the most important milk producers in Ariaal settlements, providing an average of 0.8 liters milk per person per day from the average herd, which has three milk camels for eight people. Cattle produce an average of 1.0 liters of milk each daily, ranging from 0.5 to 1.5 liters, depending on the condition of pasture and length of lactation. However, because cattle are herded away from the lowland Ariaal settlements for much of the year, they play only a minor role in settlement subsistence and mainly feed their camp herders. During wet seasons, cattle will return to the domestic settlements and contribute to the milk supply. During good periods of rainfall, cattle produce enough milk fat to make butter. Ariaal do not make cheese products.

With average household herds of three milk camels, four milk cows, and twelve milk goats and sheep, Ariaal have access to an average of 1.5 liters of milk per person daily. However, actual milk consumption varies by both seasonal supplies and by differential consumption patterns based on age, gender, and wealth differences. A warrior in a cattle camp may drink three to four liters of milk mixed with blood in one sitting, while settlement children may have access only to one liter or less of milk daily. In the dry season when milk yields are reduced, households which own only a few camels may have no milk and depend on store-bought grains to survive. The grains, usually maize-meal sometimes wheat flour, are made as porridge, consumed with milk, sugar, and butter in good times, or just plain in bad times.

Maasai and other pastoralists are renowned for their drinking of blood tapped from living animals. Among the Ariaal it is mainly warriors in livestock camps who consume blood, which is taken whole or, more often, mixed with milk. Women will eat cooked blood obtained from slaughtered animals, but avoid fresh blood which they find too rich. However women at childbirth are given blood "to gain strength," and a small stock is ritually killed to provide the mother with both physical and spiritual "strength." Blood is obtained from a living animal, usually gelded males of both large and small stock, by puncturing the jugular vein (or facial vein in a camel) with a small bow and specialized "blood" arrow. Stock are not bled more than once every three or four weeks each, yet it is estimated that a male camel will provide thirty-five liters of blood for human consumption annually.

As the dry season progresses and milk resources are depleted, meat and maize-meal are increasingly consumed as households slaughter or sell goats, sheep, and to a lesser extent cattle. Ariaal will also eat cattle or camels which have died from predation or disease. The high milk, meat, and blood diet of East African herders provides more than adequate protein, exceeding the WHO recommended protein allowances of 65 grams per adult male and 50 grams per adult women per day. Despite high protein intake among the Ariaal, daily calorie consumption is low and there are seasonal shortages, particularly at the end of the dry season when their animals are producing very little milk. Where Americans typically consume over 2500 kcal of energy per day, Ariaal and other East African pastoralists make due on less than 1600 kcal per day, and less than 1200 kcal in the dry season, which Ariaal call "the long hunger."

Nevertheless, Ariaal pastoralists with adequate herds are able to generate sufficient livestock products to offer adequate calories and more than adequate protein to each person, a feature not found among town dwellers in the same region. Despite seasonal shortages and differential consumption patterns, Ariaal livestock economy provides perhaps the optimum subsistence system available within this desert environment.

LIVESTOCK MARKETING

Ariaal livestock do not provide people with all the food they need. While Ariaal are mainly subsistence pastoralists and not commercial ranchers, they nevertheless must periodically sell livestock to purchase grains, tea, and sugar, particularly in the dry season. In 1976, Lewogoso households with average herd sizes of 35 cattle, 15 camels, and 75 small stock each, sold on average 4–5 cattle, no camels, and 12 small stock per year for a cash value of about $175. Twenty years later, I found average household herds in Lewogoso of 20 cattle, 16 camels, and 96 small stock, a decrease in cattle and increase in goats and sheep reflecting recent drought conditions. However, offtake had increased as each house was selling an average of 5 cattle, 1 camel, and 20 small stock per year, for a cash total of $655. The main reason for these increased sales was the very high cost of maize-meal, which had quadrupled in twenty years, due to the deregulation of maize prices in Kenya brought about by the conditions of the World Bank's Structural Adjustment Loans. Ariaal were selling more of their animals just to buy food, and this situation threatens to worsen. Many critics have pointed to the inequality and suffering brought about by the Structural Adjustment Programs in Africa, which includes the end to large social spending, the privatization of most businesses and enterprises, and the end to price supports and subsidies to farmers (including maize farmers). Few studies have shown the effect of these policies on pastoral populations.

While some view East African pastoralists as isolated and self-sufficient, they have traded livestock for grains for generations, if not centuries. In the nineteenth century, for example, herders in northern Kenya traded livestock products for millet, tobacco, ironware, and ornaments from Konso agriculturalists in southern Ethiopia, while LChamus agro-pastoralists around Lake Baringo in Kenya steadily supplied Swahili caravans with grains, as well as building up their herds by exchanging small stock for cattle with Somali traders. Much of the local pastoral trade was curtailed under colonial and settler rule, however. Quarantines, tribal grazing blocks, and restrictions from markets marginalized Maasai, Samburu, and Boran from the lucrative urban livestock markets, which were dominated by European ranchers. Although Kenya won independence from settler rule in 1963, this pattern of exclusion continued as private ranchers—now African and Indian as well as European—effectively kept pastoral populations on the sidelines of the growing live-stock economy. This situation is changing as pastoralist live-stock is increasingly entering the market, particularly in the south among Maasai. But overall the situation in East Africa is markedly different from West Africa, where Fulani and Tu-areg herders have been involved in regional export markets for centuries, providing seventy-five to ninety percent of all cattle and goats consumed in urban areas of the coast.

Ariaal sell 5–10% of their herds annually, mainly steers and male goats, to local or urban markets. Ariaal herders often sell animals to local Somali traders and shopkeepers, people who have lived in the region for generations. The shopkeepers offer credit to pastoral households to purchase maize-meal and other foods, collecting their debt once or twice a year when they can transport the animals down country or to larger buyers. Ariaal prefer to sell cattle at larger markets where they can fetch higher prices, and they are usually taken by foot down county to Isiolo town on the main road to Nanyuki and Nairobi. These large urban areas have a steady demand for meat, and cattle can fetch $100–$200 each, compared to small stock which bring in about $25 each.

SUMMARY

The relationship of pastoralists to their livestock herds is a complex one and determines much of the character of their society. Pastoralists depend on their animals for survival, and animals depend on their herders for grazing, water, and protection. Unlike the farmer who can tend her gardens from the same village for her whole life, pastoralists must organize household production to suit the needs of animals, which must be herded over wide areas. This leads to social organization that stresses household autonomy, mutual co-operation and defense, and the maintenance of social ties over a wide geographic area. The division of herds into domestic milk stock and surplus animals grazed in distant camps demands a structured but flexible division of labor allowing for high mobility and quick response to grazing opportunities.

The various herds have their own grazing and water requirements, and each in turn provide calories, protein, and surplus for trade to their herders. The fates of human herders and their livestock populations are interlinked, and the herder is conscious of both short-term and long-term herding requirements for their animals.

The raising of livestock for subsistence by the Ariaal, using camels for milk and transport and cattle and small stock for meat and exchange, is the most adaptive food production system in this arid environment. Agriculture, fishing, or hunting-gathering as food strategies cannot support as many people as livestock pastoralism in this region. Therefore, it appears short-sighted to alter this traditional subsistence system to suit the needs of the market, as many development agencies advocate. These changes brought about by development are discussed in more detail in Chapter 6.

5

The Clan Settlement— Basis of Ariaal Social Organization

Ariaal settlements are the center of social life. They are clan-based communities, where men are related as brothers in the same patrilineage, and where women, married from other clan villages, make their permanent home. Children call all married male elders by the same term of respect (*apayia*), address all married women as "mother" (*yeyo*), and call each other "brother" (*lalashe*) and "sister" (*ng'anashe*). The clan settlement is an extended family group and, like all families, it experiences both joy and conflict. The Ariaal (and Maasai) term for a nomadic village is *ng'ang*, meaning "ours" and meaning specifically "our family." A typical Ariaal question after greeting a stranger is *"Leng'ang era iye?,"* ("which family/clan are you from?"), which determines how one should behave (i.e., as a brother or sister, a mother or father, an in-law, or a nonrelative).

Ariaal settlements range from large lowland camel-keeping settlements of over fifty houses such as Lewogoso Lukumai, to small highland cattle-keeping homesteads of three to ten houses. Highland settlements are situated close to rich grazing and water for their cattle, and some communities can be quite large. Karare settlement on Marsabit Mountain, the village I first visited on my motorcycle in

1974, is made up of several hundred households, predominantly from the Lorokushu clan, spread in clusters along the main road to Marsabit town.

The first evening I spent in Karare, I took a walk around the large circular village, greeting women who were sitting outside their houses. It soon became very dark and I realized that I was lost. Armed with a twelve word vocabulary acquired that afternoon, I asked a woman "*Yeyo, kore ngajiai?* ('Mother, where is my house?). To my great embarrassment, the woman responded in a high voice of a young child, "Mommy, where's my house?" But with a laugh, she showed me the way back.

Both highland and lowland settlements are constructed to serve the needs of their livestock, with separate enclosures for camels, cattle, and small stock, each with pens separating nursing stock from their mothers except during milking times. Houses are arranged in a broad circle around the animal pens, and the entire village is surrounded by a thick thorn-bush fence with each house having its own "gate" of thornbush, which is pulled back to let animals in and out of the village each morning and evening. The fences are designed to keep domestic animals in and wild animals out, although it is not unusual for a hyena to jump into the small stock enclosure and leap out over the fence with a goat in its mouth before anyone can respond.

Late afternoons and early evenings are my favorite time in the village. Cattle, camels, goats, sheep, and donkeys come in from all directions at great distances, their dust trails seen for miles reflected in the setting sun, with the peaks of Baiyo Mountain or the Ndotos forming a magnificent backdrop. Elders stand outside their gates, leaning on the camel sticks as they count, admire, think, and worry about their livestock. Soon women are milking cows and goats, while young children are running around, laughing, singing, and generally excited about the approaching meal time. After everyone has eaten, people sit outdoors, particularly on moonlit evenings, when adults talk softly deep into the night. In the distance young warriors can be heard singing in their deep voices, soon joined by their girlfriends who harmonize in soprano.

Dusk is also a dangerous period, a time when animal predators can appear and attack the livestock. Once, Padamu was returning from food shopping in Ngurunit town with a loading donkey. It was getting dark and difficult to see. Suddenly, a large and fast moving body crashed into the donkey and ran off. It was a hyena, and it literally disemboweled the donkey with one bite taken on the run. Padamu hurried the donkey home, periodically pushing its dangling intestines back inside its belly. She came to my house and asked me to help, as I had a pretty complete first aid kit. I sutured the animal up, although sewing its skin was like working with shoe leather. It was my first (but not last) suture job, and the animal lived. These hazards of living near wild animals are not infrequent, and are a major reason warriors carry spears.

WOMEN'S HOUSES, WOMEN'S WORK

Each house is made by a woman, as are all the objects one finds in it. When I was collecting the time allocation data, I asked a married woman "What is women's work?" The woman replied, "Everything, everything you see here is woman's work. We make the houses, we make the roof mats, we prepare the animal hides, we milk the animals and store the milk in containers we made, we prepare the food, and we raise the children. Everything you see is the work of women. Men don't make *anything!*"

Lowland houses are large and airy, constructed both for protection from the heat as well as easy disassembly when it is time to move. The houses are made in the Rendille fashion, tall temporary structures rather than the Samburu houses, which are more permanent, low lying and heavy, and covered in mud or dung. The houses are formed by tying together strong curved roof poles with leather cords, covering on the outside with woven sisal mats and lining on the inside with cattle or camel hides. Rendille (and lowland Ariaal) houses are uniquely shaped, domed in the back and sloped in the front where the entrance door is located (see Figure 5.1).

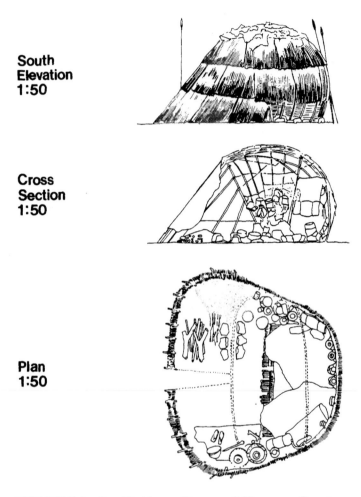

South
Elevation
1:50

Cross
Section
1:50

Plan
1:50

FIGURE 5.1 Rendille House, Diameter 3.65 meters (Drawing by Anders Grum)

The inside of each Ariaal house is remarkably similar. It is divided into a private rear half for sleeping and a 'public' front half for cooking and socializing. The two sections are separated by an oval shaped wood frame partition that can also be used to load baggage on camels or donkeys. Each house is divided into a woman's side (the area left of the door) and the man's side (to the right). The front left quarter of the house is the woman's cooking area, and includes a cooking hearth of two or three large rocks set in the ground so that it can balance a cooking pot. Firewood is usually stored near the hearth, while cooking utensils, leather bags with meal and sugar, and milk gourds are neatly tied on the wall behind the hearth. Each member of the family has her own personal milk gourd, and a mother will often tie medicine bundles or beads on the gourd to protect the individual.

The right front of the house, like the cooking area, has a dirt floor, but visitors are encouraged to sit on the husband's stool, a gift made for him at his wedding. In addition, water containers and herding and fence sticks are located near the door. More dangerous weapons, including spears (not regularly used), swords, or less frequently, bows and arrows, are tied securely to the roof frame in the rear of the house to keep out of children's hands. The rear half of the house is for sleeping, and usually consists of skins laid over soft branches and leaves. However, steel beds and mattresses are appearing with more frequency.

A major function of the house is to escape the midday heat, and the skins lining the inner wall can easily be pushed up to let in cool air. Another function of the house is to provide some privacy for cooking, eating, and quiet domestic conversations, as there are always people outside eager to engage in conversation or pass the time.

Ariaal houses are easily dismantled and loaded on a camel or donkey. Women are responsible for the creation and maintenance of all the material goods of domestic life, and it is hard to see an Ariaal woman not active in the construction or repair of some object. They carve milk containers from blocks of soft wood, weave roof mats from wild sisal gathered in the mountains, make floor mats from palm fronds, make leather skirts from goat skin and decorate them with beads. "Look around this house," a woman exclaimed, "is there anything you see that has not been made by a woman?"

One sad consequence of modernization is the disappearance of beautiful objects Ariaal once made and their replacement by store bought goods. Plastic water jugs now replace the woven sisal containers women used to store water, plastic sheets now replace woven sisal mats on the house roofs. These goods aren't even as durable or functional as the traditional items they replaced—drinking water is now warm instead of cool, and the houses are hot and smoky instead of cool and breezy.

Each woman is responsible for her own house. If a man has more than one wife (and about half of Ariaal men have 2 or more wives), co-wives place their houses next to each other and share mutual animal enclosures. Each woman has her own allotted herd of milk animals, given to her by her husband after marriage, and she knows which cows are hers to milk. Ariaal woman were often surprised to learn that my culture only permits one wife (or at least one wife at a time). They say that polygyny (marriage to more than one woman) is important, for otherwise they would have to do all the domestic work by themselves without help. Having a co-wife ensures someone can look after one's children when away on an errand, a source to borrow sugar or tobacco, and probably an ally in disputes with husbands. I noticed however that co-wives were rarely "best friends," but did share food, child care, and favors. However, a husband may favor a new wife, providing her with more money or gifts, at least in the early years of the marriage. In time, however, woman find their main interactions and satisfactions from association with other women (including co-wives) rather than the company of men. Not having their own siblings (as men do), women form close and lasting relations with other women in the village, all of whom come from diverse clans and locations. Co-wives however may have more difficult relationships, as they are often different in age (a new bride may be 16 years old while the first wife may be 15 to 30 years older), and their may be jealousies if the husband gives more money or spends more time with a new bride.

THE CLAN SETTLEMENTS

As described in Chapter 3, Ariaal settlements are composed primarily of patrilineally related men and their families, typically organized into lineage groups whose members can trace descent to a common ancestor and share common family names. Women marry into the settlement and are not members of their husbands' clans. However, her children are members of their father's descent group, and a married woman lives within her husband's clan village until her death. If a man takes a second or third wife, she seldom comes from the same clan as his other wives, as marriage is seen as an alliance with different clan settlements which helps broaden one's social networks and with it, access to a variety of herding environments.

A small number of the settlement's population are related by marriage ties, that is, sons-in-law and brothers-in-law to the resident male stock owner. These living situations may be temporary or they may be permanent. Occasionally a Rendille brother-in-law will move into an Ariaal settlement to seek other opportunities in raising livestock, such as cattle or goats, than those offered in his own settlement. Sometimes a person wholly unrelated will join an Ariaal community, gaining an invitation based on ties of friendship. This was the case with the *laibon* Lekati Leaduma who joined Lugi's group to practice his medicine among camel keepers.

Ariaal have a history of welcoming in strangers. An example is Arge, a young Rendille who moved into Lewogoso in 1976 with his wife and mother in order to build up his small stock, cattle, and camel herds. By 1985, he had increased his herds to over 100 camels, gained a second wife, and enlarged his family from one to eight children. In time, Arge moved out of the settlement and into Ngurunit town, where he worked for the UNESCO-IPAL project herding livestock, while independently engaging in his own livestock transactions in the cash market. By 1990, Arge's family had grown to three wives and twelve children. In addition to livestock transactions, he conducted camel-back tours for tourists and had gained a reputation as a hard working and enterprising elder. Arge stands at one end of the Ariaal scale, a self-made man who was able to build up his own herds and family. At the other end of the scale lie those Ariaal with few animals, many of whom also end up in Ngurunit town searching for the few wage jobs or even becoming Dorrobo, poor people who hunt and collect honey in the mountains. Despite the appearance of equality, Ariaal households do show variation in terms of wealth measured by livestock holdings.

Within each clan settlement, households join together to form cooperative herding groups to share labor and mutual production tasks in the herding camps. This cooperation is usually organized by direct kinship ties, such as the families of two brothers, but sometimes they form by individual choice, independent of kinship relations, based on compatibility and mutual need. Cooperative herding groups, whether based on kinship or not, tend to be fluid and fluctuate according to the particular needs of households for labor or access to milk stock.

POLITICS AND CONFLICT RESOLUTION

In anthropological usage, politics may be defined as the process by which decisions affecting the larger social group are made, rules for group behavior established, competition for positions of leadership regulated, and the disruptive effects of disputes minimized. As with other kinship-based, non-state polities, Ariaal have internal processes of governance and conflict resolution without having formal institutions of chiefs, courts, judges, or police. Ariaal, like other Kenyan citizens, do fall under the judicial laws of the state, and will be arrested and go to court if they commit crimes of theft, assault, and murder. But many of the conflicts of everyday life such as disputes between kinsmen or neighbors within the group, as well as relations with outsiders, are resolved by their own rules of internal governance and mediation. Ariaal have no traditional chiefs or headman, rather every married male elder has an equal voice in village affairs. Even unmarried warriors and women can make their opinions known in the large general discussions periodically held in the village. Elders try to resolve conflicts by argument and consensus, where all, or at least the vocal majority, agree on a course of action. When a conflict or dispute is resolved, the elders will invariably hold public blessings that ask God (n'gai) to protect the village or community from further harm.

Community politics are divided into two arenas: keeping peace within the clan settlement, and dealing with outsiders who may be friends and kinsmen (Ariaal, Samburu, and Rendille), enemies (Boran, Turkana), or neutrals (shopkeepers, government officials, Europeans, and the like). Internal relations among Ariaal are defined and regulated by the two organizing principles of clan affiliation and the age-set organization. Relations with other Ariaal, Rendille, or Samburu communities are treated as an internal community who share kinship affiliation. Disputes nevertheless arise, such as competition over grazing or water holes, or more often, disputes between the warrior groups of different clan settlements. The disputes of warriors are often over girlfriends, and on occasion turn violent. Warriors from Lewogoso Lukumai have long been in dispute with Longieli clan, which occasionally comes to blows. When fights do break out, the elders of both communities come together to resolve the conflict, often castigating warriors of their own clans, and calling for peace with both fines and ritual blessings. If a homicide among kinsmen occurs, it is treated with horror, even if it is accidental. A "blood price" is paid to the family of the deceased, which can reach up to 40 cattle, collected from kinsmen of the murderer. The stigma of murder is very high, where the perpetuator may leave the community; some have even committed suicide.

A more common internal dispute is that between full brothers, and often jealousy lies at the heart of the problem. Although rarely violent, I did witness one incident in Lewogoso settlement where two brothers (both in the Mekuri age-set initiated in 1937), came to blows. These two men had a continuous rivalry based ultimately on the younger brother's success in stock management, which made him the wealthier of the two. Furthermore, the younger brother had two wives while the older had only one. In this particular incident, the older brother ordered his brother's younger wife to run errands for him at Ngurunit, a round trip of thirty kilometers. When the younger brother returned home to discover his wife gone, he complained loudly to his older brother and told him not to interfere with him or his household. The argument got more heated and the older brother hit the younger one in the head with his camel stick, causing bloodshed (and my administering three stitches over his eye). Overt violence between kinsmen is a serious offense among Ariaal, and the elders disapproved of the two brothers fighting. They publicly intervened, separating the two brothers, and called for a meeting that night. They upheld fraternal seniority by fining the younger brother a goat and payment for beer (a peace gesture) because he had shouted at his older brother, starting the argument in the first place. Prayers were said, and the situation quieted down. However, the settlement elders privately agreed that the younger brother's actions were just, and the older brother, disgraced, moved away and joined another clan settlement. Fission, or separation of households from each other, is a feature of nomadic society that helps resolve conflict in the absence of higher authority.

Conflict between different pastoralist groups, while nothing new in northern Kenya, has heated up dramatically in the past ten years. Warfare between northern Kenyan pastoralists, particularly Turkana and Boran against the Ariaal, Samburu, and Rendille, is a strongly shared experience, caused mainly by competition for grazing land or the need to capture cattle and other livestock. All of these groups tell stories of great battles and wars between them, and these societies are well known for mobilizing groups of armed men quickly to raid or counter-raid each other. These groups feel no kinship for each other, in fact they barely recognize each other as fellow human beings. The concept of homicide, where a blood price is paid, does not hold towards enemy tribes, and killing an enemy is treated with honor. Ariaal and Rendille wear a brass bracelet on their wrist to show how many enemies they have killed in battle.

Through large-scale warfare occurred unfettered in the 19th century peace between pastoral groups in Marsabit and elsewhere in the first half of the 20th century was maintained by colonial rule. However, following independence in 1963, groups in Northeastern Kenya including Somalis and Boran attempted to secede and join Somalia, a move that was harshly put down by the Kenyan government. Starved and brutalized, raiders from Somali and Boran (known as *shifta*, or bandits) attacked Rendille and Ariaal for cattle. They responded in force to fight the *shiftas* as described by Kitoip's experiences in Chapter 2. More recently, warfare has re-erupted in the poorly policed areas of northern Kenya. During the extensive droughts of the 1990s, livestock raids increased, particularly by Turkana against Samburu but also by groups who hitherto had not bothered anyone, such as Gabra who attacked Boran, Dasenech, and Rendille in 1992. Most recently, attacks have increased between Boran and Rendille settled on farms in Marsabit Mountain, taking the form of attacks against unarmed women walking on the road to market. In this situation, development organizations including GTZ and religious NGOs organized mediation between Boran and Rendille elders, both of whom said the problem was with their young warriors, who they needed to better control. Where population growth and competition for resources is a leading factor of war, the situation is complicated by the increase in small arms into the area from neighboring Ethiopia, Somali, and Sudan, and by the poor security afforded to pastoralists living away from the towns.

LEWOGOSO LUKUMAI SETTLEMENT

Lewogoso Lukumai is typical of the large lowland Ariaal clan settlements. The community ranges in size from a single large circle of over fifty houses to several circles spread apart from each other depending on variations in vegetation, age-set ritual calendar, and political insecurities. In 1976, Lewogoso's members were living near Baiyo Mountain in one large settlement of 250 people living in fifty-two houses and keeping 600 camels, 800 cattle, and 2000 goats and sheep. The settlement consisted of eight lineage groups (Lengesen, Leriare, Letapo, Lenkiribe, Lenampere, Lebaiyo, Lesinkopana, and Leboinyo), spatially distributed as shown in Figure 5.2. In 2000, the settlement had grown and split

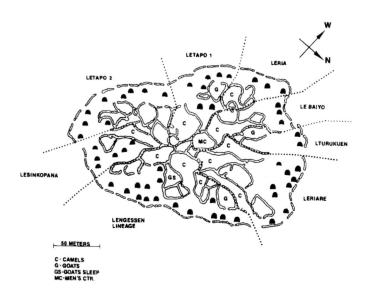

FIGURE 5.2 Lineage groupings in Lewogoso Lukumai settlement

into several sections, having grown in both human and live-stock populations.

Ariaal settlements are fluid, where households will come together and separate, depending mainly on environmental conditions. In 1976 all households were able to live together, herding their cattle in distant highland camps and living off their large camel herds. However, by 1985 following the 1984 famine, Lewogoso had separated into four communi-ties. Those with large camel herds remained near Baiyo Mountain, and those with fewer camels but more cattle and small stock lived closer to the Ngurunit wells. A third com-munity, made up mainly of cattle and small stock keepers, moved 50 kilometers southwest, higher into the Ndoto Mountains at Losidan for the better grazing and water re-sources. A fourth community developed in Ngurunit town, made up primarily of poorer Ariaal with few animals. The entire community came together in one large circle for the circumcision rituals of the Moli age-set in 1992, but soon after separated into the same four communities again. Livestock ownership per household remained fairly consistent with 1976 levels, and in some cases had grown, a fact I attribute to the outmigration of poorer herders to the towns and farms.

HOUSEHOLDS AND THE ORGANIZATION OF PRODUCTION

Life in the settlements revolves around daily herding needs of the domestic livestock. Individual households cooperate extensively with each other in watering and grazing of their herds, both from the domestic settlements and in the distant livestock camps. Each household keeps its livestock within its own animal enclosure, separated by species and often by age, with nursing stock confined to their own enclosures to keep them from nursing at will. Co-wives recognize their own milk animals, which may be mixed in the same enclosure, but they cooperate with each other in milking and herding tasks. Different households will join force in mutual assistance, particularly those of the same lineage who usually share the same side of the settlement (a lineage is a subgroup of the clan who can trace ancestry to a common grandfather, often sharing the same family name). Large clan settlements are made up of several lineages, as in Lewogoso where Lengesen, Letapo Leria, and Leriare are prominent families.

An Ariaal household may be defined as the smallest domestic group with its own livestock and which makes decisions over allocation of labor and livestock capital. Households may be separated. A stock owner may leave one wife in a highland area with cattle, a second wife in a small town where some children go to school, or another in the lowlands with the camels and small stock. More often, households stay together and consist of a married man and his wife or co-wives, children, and dependents such as a widowed mother or mother-in-law or married daughter who has not yet joined her husband's village. Young widows with unmarried children constitute their own household where the woman holds the household herds in trust until her sons are mature enough to take control of their animals, although sometimes the late husband's brothers will try to take control of the herds. But a woman's control of livestock is temporary. Once her sons marry the herds are divided up, and she must depend on one of her sons, usually the youngest, with whom she lives.

Households change in size and composition over time, experiencing different problems at each stage. A young couple will have few or no children, and must perform most of the herding, milking, and watering tasks themselves. As the household matures, additional labor is provided by co-wives and adolescent children, offering the largest ratio of workers to the household. Finally as these children marry and begin their own households, the original couple (or surviving widow or less common widower) find declining labor again a problem, and will often become dependent on their children's households.

Because households are self-sufficient units, they must provide their own labor to manage their own animals. Ariaal solve problems of labor shortages through a variety of mechanisms. If a household has too few animals and too many people, it may borrow milk stock from wealthier kin; send excess labor away, either to herd for wealthier families or to migrate to urban centers in search of wage labor or school; merge its herds with other families and share the labor and food within the context of the livestock camps; or combine these processes.

Conversely, if the household size is too small to manage its animals, which might happen with a wealthy but small family, it may merge its herds with another to share labor; hire extra labor, usually from a large, poor, and related family within the settlement in exchange for payment in livestock; or lend or place livestock elsewhere, usually with a relative in another settlement.

Ariaal households, while fundamentally similar and egalitarian as in other small and kinship based societies, have a great deal of variation in size, composition, and levels of wealth from different livestock holdings. An example is the household of La'amo, a hardworking but poor junior elder with a young wife and two small children. Because his children were small, La'amo herded his small stock by himself, while his camels were grazed with a wealthier kinsman. This contrasts with the household of Lesupir, a young elder but considerably richer than La'amo. Lesupir was the eldest son of a wealthy family with a large herd of camels and small stock. He solved his labor problems by recruiting his two younger warrior brothers to herd his camels.

Finally, there is the household of Ukarre, a man in his late 60s who has two wives and eleven children ranging in ages from nine months to thirty two years old. Ukarre owned 26 cattle, 38 camels, and over 70 small stock, managing them all with his own household labor. Ukarre represents an Ariaal ideal of an elder owning sufficiently large numbers of animals and a large domestic labor force to care for them.

Comparing forty-five households, I found that members of poor households did not necessarily work harder than wealthy ones, as poor families had few animals, while rich households with many animals had higher labor needs. Sometimes they hired additional labor, or they had enough wealth to marry second wives and produce more children. Members of households that owned more small stock than large animals worked considerably harder than households with large cattle and camel herds, and members of younger households with small children worked harder than older families with larger numbers of adolescent children. In a finding that surprised me, married women from wealthier households worked harder than poorer women for, although they had additional herding labor, they had to perform more milking tasks. Furthermore, these women put any free time into manufacturing prestige goods such as woven roof mats and beaded skirts. Less surprisingly, men from older and wealthier households worked less intensely than men from smaller and poorer households, and across the board married men had more rest or leisure time than women.

Variation in Household Wealth

As illustrated above, Ariaal households display great variation in size, composition of their members, and wealth despite an appearance of homogeneity and conformity. Due to both changes in the developmental cycle of the domestic group and actual differences in inherited and acquired wealth, there is a range of differences in wealth: poor households may not have enough animals to feed their members and wealthy households may lack adequate labor to manage all their animals. Wealthier families hire poor relatives to herd their animals, paying one heifer cow or camel to boys working in the satellite camps for one year, or one small stock to younger boys or girls helping herd small stock near the domestic settlement. Poor but unrelated households may foster or loan a child to a wealthier household to herd animals in exchange for the payment of an animal after a year's service. Old widows without any stock will be given a milk animal, or a gourd of milk, each day by a relative, and everyone is free to "beg" or borrow food from kinsmen.

Despite these wealth differences, there exists a strong "ethos of egalitarianism" and reciprocity. Kinship obligations provides a context for sharing, leading to a redistribution of milk animals with wealthy families loaning animals to poorer kin. Furthermore, households create cooperative herding arrangements to accommodate variations and shortages in livestock and/or labor, such that those families with too few children or laborers can foster or hire other children to herd their animals in exchange for livestock gifts.

During our health and nutrition studies of the 1990s, we saw that the "moral economy" or redistribution and reciprocity was breaking down among settled Rendille and Ariaal living in both towns and on farms. Women and children in the pastoral community of Lewogoso showed no differences in weights, mid-arm circumferences (which measure muscle mass) and triceps skinfolds (which measure adipose fat content in the upper arm) based on wealth differences—both wealthy and poor households consumed similar amounts and types of food. However, in the agricultural community of Songa, wealthier women (of which there were few) had greater dietary intakes of *posho*, greens, and beans, while poorer women sold off most of their nutritious foods and lived on *posho* and smaller amounts of greens alone.

While many households risk losing livestock during drought, heavy rains, or raids, losses are not endured equally. Rich households retain a larger number of animals than poor families. A herd owner of 100 animals can survive and recover after losses of 50%, while one with 10 animals cannot survive such a loss. This creates an increased polarization of wealth following crises, and although observers usually point to the leveling effects of periodic climatic stress, they in fact divided Ariaal society into those who are able to remain pastoralists and those who cannot. Following large losses in the droughts of 1984, 1992, and 1996–97, about 10% of Ariaal stock owners moved out of the pastoral economy altogether, settling in towns of Ngurunit and Laisamis. Nevertheless, most Ariaal households were able to survive these droughts, and continue their pastoral existence to this day.

SOCIAL DIFFERENTIATION AND INCIPIENT STRATIFICATION

Ariaal do not constitute a class-based society, at least not in their internal relationships. Elders no more form a fixed "nonproducing" class than youth and warriors form an impoverished "producing" class, although this may change as Ariaal become more involved in commercial livestock sales, as among Maasai in southern Kenya where rich "big men" are emerging. But Ariaal elders do hold a privileged position in the society—they work less and own more property than any other group. Furthermore, it can be argued that they do appropriate some of the products of their dependent juniors and women. The prolonged period of warriorhood allows elders to keep their household labor force by delaying the marriage of their warrior sons until their midthirties. However, where warriors become elders, marry, raise their own animals, or inherit their father's animals, women never do.

Social stratification is not unknown in pastoralist societies, particularly in the Mideast and southwest Asia, where pastoral societies are characterized by chieftain hierarchies, state incorporation, and pronounced patron-client relationships. In these societies, relationships are established between members of poor households and those of wealthier households, often in the context of ritual and kinship ties. Often these relationships translate into exploitative ones as wealthier households use the labor power of poorer households without returning an equivalent share of the product.

A similar trend of class formation appears to be emerging among East African pastoralists, as exemplified in recent developments among Maasai described in Chapter 2. Affected by drought, development, and the political turmoil, many former pastoralists are migrating to towns to seek wage labor if poor, or participate in the growing livestock market as entrepreneurs if wealthy or educated. Ultimately, a new class of educated and more privileged entrepreneurs is developing, with rural and poorer kin becoming proletarianized as wage-laborers and clients.

Wage relations do not yet dominate Ariaal economy, but the market economy is expanding into Ariaal, accelerated by the process of drought, national development plans, and the activities of international development agencies. Ariaal society, traditionally divided into wealthier and poorer households, is currently experiencing a separation between those who can remain in the pastoral livestock economy and those who cannot. Not all town dwellers are poor, however, as there is emerging a new elite of livestock traders, store owners, and a "salariat" of government-employed administrators drawn from the pastoralist community among Ariaal, Samburu, and Rendille. As sedentarization and modern education proceed in northern Kenya, irreversible stratification will proceed with it, leading to a polarization of Ariaal that has already begun among Maasai, Boran, and Samburu societies.

I remain amazed at how little Lewogoso Lukumai community has changed in twenty-five years. When I visited Lewogoso in July 1996 and conducted my livestock surveys and questionnaires among elders about their year, I found that people were herding their animals in the same areas as before, that the same small numbers of Ariaal were dropping out of the pastoral society and migrating to towns, and that households were selling roughly the same number of animals they were twenty years ago. One major difference, however, was that the number of Lewogoso families increased from fifty-two households to seventy-three households. Population densities of the Ariaal living away from towns are still sufficiently low and their pastures are not as yet degraded. Clearly, livestock pastoralism continues to provide the most certain food production system in this arid region, and Ariaal pastoralists remain a viable and vibrant society.

6

Farms, Towns, and the Future of the Ariaal

Life for Kenya's pastoralists has changed substantially, if not irreversibly, in the last twenty five years. Increasingly many Ariaal as well as Rendille, Boran, Samburu, and Maasai have settled in or near permanent towns, abandoning or severely modifying their former pastoral lives. While the majority of people, at least 80% of Ariaal and 50% of the Rendille, continue to live with and subsist off their livestock, about 4000 Rendille and Ariaal have taken up agriculture or agro-pastoralism (raising livestock and crops together) on Marsabit Mountain. Nearly half of the Rendille (about 12,000 people) have moved near two mission towns of Korr and Kargi in the lowlands, to receive famine foods or escape areas of warfare.

Several factors have contributed to this sedentarization process. Population growth, the loss of herding range, increasing drought and risks to their livestock herds, and increased raiding by pastoral neighbors have acted as "pushes", while the attraction of schools, hospitals, famine-relief foods, and new economic opportunities have acted as "pulls." This situation is not very different from other areas of Africa where rural to urban migration is steadily increasing. Not all of these settled townspeople are impoverished, nor have all given up their ties to their rural communities.

For pastoralists, settled life presents many new opportunities formerly unavailable including farming, dairy marketing, increased livestock marketing, education for their children and wage labor for the adults.

Sedentarization, the settling down of former nomads, is not new to the Ariaal, nor indeed to many other East African pastoralist groups. Farming, foraging, and fishing were options pursued by even the most specialized pastoralists such as the Maasai in the past, particularly during periods of famine, war, or ecological stress. Marsabit Mountain has been home to Samburu speaking Ariaal since at least the mid-nineteenth century, where living in permanent settlements, they took their cattle to forest water points and even kept camels, who could grazed on mountainside pastures kept free of ticks by regular burning. However, the settling of former pastoralists has increased dramatically on Marsabit Mountain, whose population has grown from 4000 in 1975 to 30,000 today, nearly one third of the entire district's residents. Furthermore, much of this settling has been encouraged by international aid donors, relief organizations, and churches, who have developed agricultural projects on the mountain.

THE GROWTH OF TOWNS AND MISSIONS

Towns developed slowly in northern Kenya, for the colonial British government purposely kept the district undeveloped so that it could serve as a military buffer against an expansionist Ethiopia to the north and Italian Somalia to the east. A major road from Isiolo in the south to Moyale on the Ethiopian border was built in the 1930s, and the British attracted Boran herders and Burji agriculturalists to Marsabit to provide milk and crops for the work crews and police. Soon, Somali and Meru traders arrived building shops around these posts and small towns began to develop. The district capital of Marsabit town was only 400 people in 1933, reaching 2500 by 1963.

At the time of Kenyan independence in 1963, Marsabit District's 80,000 people had two major towns (Marsabit and

Moyale) and several small towns at Archer's Post, Laisamis, and Loglogo on the Marsabit road. The district had only three primary schools, no secondary schools, and one government hospital. The Kenya government under Jomo Kenyatta made little investment in the north, allocating most resources and development funds to the densely populated regions down country. President Daniel Arap Moi, who succeeded Kenyatta at his death in 1978, made more gestures to develop resources in the north, as he depended on the support of Kenya's smaller agro-pastoral groups like Samburu and Rendille to maintain the political power of his own small group (Kalenjin) against more numerous Kikuyu, Luo, and Swahili. By 2000, Marsabit District (now separated from Moyale to the north) had 138,500 people, 7 secondary schools, 54 primary schools, 4 hospitals, 15 medical dispensaries. Towns lying both on the major road (including Merille, Laisamis, Karare) as well as those on the road from Marsabit town to Lake Turkana (Maikona, North Horr, Loyangalanai) have all grown in size, while rural areas have seen developments in particularly in water projects (mechanizing wells, building dams and catchments, and in some locations, piping water for irrigated agriculture). These road towns are economically active with shops and markets for pastoralists selling livestock.

A significant amount of Marsabit's development was provided by international religious donors, particularly the Roman Catholic Church and Protestant organizations including the African Inland Church (AIC), World Vision, and Food for the Hungry. Unlike Maasai land which had substantial investments by the United States Agency for International Development (USAID), the only major bilateral (county to country) international aid was provided by Germany's state development agency GTZ, which was active in agricultural and pastoral projects in the district during the 1990s.

The Catholic Church has been one of the most important agencies of development in the area. Since 1954 and particularly after the drought of the 1973 established twelve missions with churches, primary schools and dispensaries, as well as a hospital in Laisamis and a secondary school in

Marsabit town. Following the Sahelian Famine (1968–1973), the Marsabit Catholic Diocese began distributing famine relief foods (principally maize, soy, and powdered milk donated by the United States government), using church vehicles and staff to reach out to destitute nomads in the Rendille, Boran, and Gabra areas. In the Rendille area, the towns of Korr and Kargi sprung up from desert water points where Catholic missionaries distributed grains, later becoming permanent towns with mechanized wells and permanent churches and schools. By the 1980s these centers had attracted traders and a large numbers of impoverished Rendille, who today number about 12,000, one half of the Rendille population.

Unlike towns lying on the main road such as Laisamis and Karare which have lively economic activity, the mission towns of Korr and Kargi are depressing to live in. Both are located in wind-swept and barren desert areas, and neither have enough vegetation to support animal herds. Permanent residents include a core of about 1000 in each town, with another 3–4000 Rendille living in settlements within 10 kilometers. Living in barren settlements while their animals are herded elsewhere, the Rendille depend on either famine-relief foods or store-bought foods acquired from selling their animals. While these towns do have churches, schools, and dispensaries, there are few jobs available. Most shops are run by Somalis or other non-Rendille, as Rendille would have a hard time demanding payment from their neighbors and relatives. Alcoholism is a growing problem for Rendille men and women who have little to do, where illegal beer brewing is associated with prostitution and the increasing risk of HIV/AIDS.

The Rendille have been attracted to the mission towns to a much greater degree than the Ariaal. In part this is because the Catholic church focused its massive famine-relief efforts in the Rendille and Gabra areas, ignoring the more isolated Ariaal communities. Moreover, the flexible herding strategy of the Ariaal allowed them to move with their cattle, camels, and small stock and escape the pressures endured by Rendille, who are more constrained in the Kaisut lowlands with their predominately camel herds. Ariaal did not escape missionizing influence altogether, however, as the African Inland Church in particular concentrated on water development in Ngrunit in the Ndotos Mountains and on the agricultural community of Songa on Mt. Marsabit. They also run small schools and clinics, as well as maintain a hospital on Mt. Kulal and secondary school in Kijabe near Nairobi.

Both missions readily admit that their main work is religious conversion. The Catholic Church achieves this through primary and secondary education and large Sunday services, the smaller AIC through religious education and adult bible reading and translation classes. The church missions, like the Kenyan government as a whole, would like to see most nomads settle down. A Catholic priest in Korr told me,

> "These Rendille are really children, here today, gone tomorrow. They have no roots, no home to call their own. Here they have for the first time a regular water supply, sanitary latrines, shops, schools, a dispensary. But they have a long way to go before they can be truly independent."

Where the Catholic Church concentrates on famine-relief, the AIC's Calvinist values of self-reliance and savings inhibit them from promoting food-aid. "We want to make men of them, not babies," said an AIC missionary. Not surprisingly, the AIC have won few converts compared to the Catholic Diocese, but to their credit they have not created large communities of dependent households.

A positive aspect of this outlook on self-reliance is the AIC's experimentation with programs increasing food production, including both the restocking of small stock to impoverished pastoralists, and the introduction of farming techniques to populations living in highland areas. The restocking of animals is looked at with great favor by Ariaal. "Give me two animals and I can become a rich man," goes an Ariaal saying. However, most restocking programs offer goats rather than expensive cattle and camels, and since small stock are the first type of animal to be eaten or sold during drought, poor recipients often stay poor. Agriculture has been more successful, especially on Marsabit Mountain where several church run schemes are located.

Farming Communities on Marsabit Mountain

In 1973, the AIC and the National Christian Council of Kenya, a Protestant organization, initiated several agricultural settlement schemes for impoverished Rendille pastoralists on the southern side of Marsabit Mountain at Songa, Nasikakwe (Karare), and Kituruni. Similar efforts were initiated for Boran at Gudas and Badasa on the northern side of the mountain. Two of the schemes, Naskikakwe and Kituruni, are located near the Ariaal settlement at Karare, about 17 km south of Marsabit town, which was the first Ariaal community I visited in 1974, described in Chapter 1. Both farming schemes near Karare are located in dry areas whose maize crops depend on rainfall to grow. A different situation exists in Songa, which is located deep in the highland forest reserve 15km south of Marsabit town on a different road. With its higher concentration of water pools, AIC missionaries introduced drip irrigation, which utilizes flat plastic hoses with small holes that can provide moisture to gardens slowly without evaporation. The Songa community is green and verdant, and resembles down-country farms in Kikuyu or Meru.

Although I had initial doubts that Rendille could become productive farmers, I was greatly surprised to see in the 1990s that all three communities were successful, and densely settled with neat farms producing maize, beans, kale, tomatoes, peppers, fruit trees and fuel-wood trees. Several NGOs including Food for the Hungry and World Vision, as well as GTZ, had focused on these communities as solutions to drought and famine in the area, and had invested considerable time, expertise, and equipment in helping the communities develop. As part of development projects, many settled families were allocated iron-sheet houses and farm plots ranging from two to five acres. Each scheme offered communally shared oxen used for ploughing. Today, residents of Songa and Nasikakwe earn livings by growing subsistence crops (maize and kale) and selling surplus vegetables and tobacco in the central marketplace at Marsabit town.

Life for Rendille and Ariaal has changed dramatically for those who have taken up farming. Anthropologist Kevin Smith reports about changes in male power, particularly a decline in the collective authority of male elders, and woman's greater autonomy to grow and sell crops. Geographers Adano Wario Roba and Karen Witsenburg who have carried out extensive research among all settled communities on Marsabit Mountain report that residents of Marsabit's agricultural schemes were highly satisfied with life as farmers and few wished to return to their former pastoral lives. Farms were seen as advantageous because they provided steady food and were less risky than dependence on animals which can be lost to drought, diseases, and war. Furthermore, settled life gave opportunities for the poor, 'When you work hard, you can become independent'. But people also noted that farm work was far more onerous and that they missed the milk and meat of pastoral life.

Today, Nasikakwe and Kituruni have 1500 Rendille and Ariaal residents, and Songa has over 2000. The Boran agricultural communities were similarly successful. However, these communities face problems of both environmental and political nature. Their success has attracted a continuing stream of Rendille and Boran immigrants, threatening a water and fuelwood supply of finite quantity. Conflicts over water and farmland have intensified between the Boran and Rendille at Songa, where since 1992 a dozen people, mainly women and children, have been killed in ambushes. While elders from both communities, as well as government officials and NGOs have worked at mediating between the two groups, competition and conflict remain a continuing threat on Marsabit Mountain.

Korr town

The Impact of Towns on Ariaal Life

About one quarter of Rendille and Ariaal have become permanent town dwellers, some finding decent employment and housing; others less fortunate search for odd jobs such as cleaning and herding stock to make ends meet. Many town residents have converted to Christianity, some to Islam; most still adhere to many Rendille and Samburu customs of age-sets, marriage, and blessings. Despite these major changes, Ariaal are not opposed to these new influences. Ariaal see the towns as one more resource to utilize, an essential alternative for poor households who have few animals, or an important center to gain employment, sell livestock, seek health care, and obtain education for their children.

Patrick Ngoley, a resident of Korr town, told me:

Before we were nomads, we would move with our animals. Now we stay in one place, at Korr or at Kargi. This is *mandeleo* [development]. Here we have shops, schools, hospitals. But we still keep our animals in *fora*. When we need money for food we tell our warriors to sell stock at Laisamis, Isiolo, or Merille. They sell them and send us home money.

But now everybody is paying for things they used to get for free—meat, transportation, *posho* [meal], milk. People must spend money until rain comes [and animals with milk can return]. People must look for work in town making buildings, cleaning houses, even digging urinals. If there is no work, people must sell an animal. If a person is too poor and has no animals or money, he must beg from others.

The new towns have attracted poor people, particularly widowed women who are not in strong situations in the no-madic villages.

Other women come to town for increased opportunities. Mairo, a woman aged 50, is the wife of a blind man and works for the local school teacher as cook and baby-sitter. She owns some animals (including five milk cows, which are grazed by her sons). She describes her life:

> Before in Longieli [a nomadic clan village], life was not bad, but it is much better here in Ngurunit. I don't have to go far for water or firewood. Also this place is safer for my husband. I can earn some money and help feed my husband. Even when cattle come here, I only have to help water them, I don't have to take them to camp, to herd them. Even when livestock are here, even if I sell a goat, I am right in town and I don't have to wait for my sons to return some time later. I found work in Ngurunit just by looking. First I worked for a Somali man, I washed his clothes, cooked, cleaned house, and fetched water. I earned 150 shillings a month, plus food [about six dollars a month]. Then bandits came and tried to steal from the Somali family. They took money, sugar, clothes from the shop—there was nobody to stop them, they were fierce and would kill you, so we all ran away. The Somali family got scared and moved back to Korr.
>
> Then I just struggled with my animals, and we stayed here. In a short while I heard of another Rendille family here, the school teacher, and I saw them

making a kitchen. I came to help and finished making their kitchen. Then the teacher's wife said, do you need a job, why don't you stay with me and help me with my children? So I stay now and earn 200 shillings a month [eight dollars], plus food for myself and husband, plus clothing. Some men oppose their wives to work for money, maybe they think we will overlook them and become proud, or we might leave them and go away with other men. With some people, this will happen.

THE HEALTH COSTS OF SETTLING DOWN

Despite the attractions of town life, it is not clear that towns provide more long term food security than nomadic life, particularly as sedentarized pastoralists are often alienated from their animals, their main source of food and livelihood. Although many development organizations as well as African governments in the arid lands see the settling of nomadic pastoralists and their conversion to commercial livestock producers as the key to a secure life, I am not convinced that the benefits of settled life outweigh the costs of abandoning traditional livestock production. In the 1990s, I and my colleagues Martha Nathan, MD and Eric Abella Roth began a long term project to monitor the health, nutrition, and wellbeing of Rendille and Ariaal women and children in town and pastoral settings. In a continuous three year study, we monitored 200 women and their 488 children every two months for daily diet, monthly morbidity (illnesses), and anthropometric measurements (heights, weights, mid-arm circumferences) in five separate communities—Lewogoso pastoralists, Korr famine-relief town, Ngurunit, small and isolated mountain town in the Ndoto Mountains, Karare agro-pastoralist community, and Songa agricultural village.

Our research found that children living in all of the settled communities had smaller body mass indices (BMI calculated as weight/height squared) than children living in pastoral Lewogoso. In fact, when we calculated the proportion of *severely* malnourished children in any community (defined as those whose BMI falls 2 standard deviations be-low, or 80% of, the World Health Organization mean), nearly one quarter (23%) of Korr's children were severely malnour-ished compared to 6% of Lewogoso's children, even during periods of drought or low rainfall. We believe that pastoral children are better nourished than town children because of their access to milk (and particularly camel's milk), and bet-ter nutrition is correlated with better health because of the body's ability to respond to infectious disease like malaria or measles is much greater in well nourished than malnour-ished children. Nevertheless, although town children have access to health clinics providing both vaccinations and cri-sis interventions, they have higher morbidity rates than the pastoral children, and which may be caused by, and contrib-utors to, their poorer nutritional status.

Our study led to several conclusions:

Not All Pastoralists Settle

People leaving the pastoral economy to settle in towns or farms are either the poorest or the richest individuals and households. The poor leave because they can no longer sup-port themselves, despite sharing and redistribution within the traditional economy. These people tend to be young adults or the elderly. Wealthier people leave to either man-age their herds from the comfort and security of town, hir-ing poorer relatives to herd for them, or to engage in other business activities, such as shopkeeping or truck transport of animals. Sedentarized communities, furthermore, are dif-ferentiated into rich and poor households to a much greater degree than pastoral communities.

Not All Marketing Behavior Is Equal

Some pastoral communities have better access to markets and are more integrated than others. Karare residents, with large cattle herds, sell many more large animals than low-land pastoralists near Korr and Ngurunit, who sell mainly small stock. Those with access to roads and markets sell more products, both dairy and vegetable, than isolated communities.

Not Everyone Benefits Equally from Town Life

While towns offer more employment and education opportunities, these are not shared equally. In addition to differences between rich and poor, gender and age differences are played out. For example, boys are three times as likely as girls to attend school, and educated youth are more likely to find work than noneducated adults.

Town or Farm Life Is Not Necessarily Beneficial to the Health and Nutrition of Children

Pastoral communities with sufficient livestock herds appear to have better nutrition and health than town or farm residents, although they suffer much more seasonal shortages than town and farm families. However, settled populations have better access to vaccinations and health care interventions.

DEVELOPMENT APPROACHES TO PASTORALISM

Sedentarization is a process that is occurring rapidly among pastoral populations throughout Africa. Among Ariaal and Rendille of Kenya, sedentism and commoditization has increased in the past twenty five years, brought about by drought, population growth, expansion of the national and international markets, as well as the development programs of international agencies including the Catholic Relief Services, GTZ, and NGOs that have come to Marsabit District. Faced with economic, ecological, and political pressures, pastoralists will respond with a variety of strategies including the adoption of cultivation, increased livestock or crop marketing, urban migration, wage labor, and a variety of strategies in between.

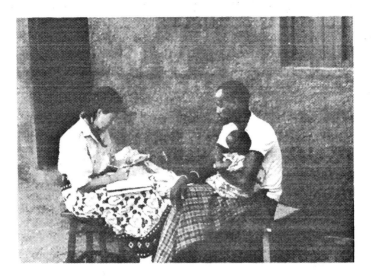

Marty Nathan, MD interviews Larian Aliyaro about his daughter's health in Korr.

However, development policies aimed at settling pasto-ralists down and integrating them wholesale into the cash market entail certain risks. Commercial ranching benefits only a small percentage of pastoralists, while wage labor is often at the lowest rungs of the employment ladder, such as the jobs of Maasai night watchmen in Nairobi. Some devel-opment efforts have focused on improving pastoralists' abil-ity to feed themselves, either by restocking animals or demonstrating improved farming techniques for those who have taken up agriculture. But the resources of Marsabit District are too dry and limited to support much of the pop-ulation with farming. Restocking, as well as the dispensing of inexpensive veterinary medicines, are ideas welcomed by pastoralists, but the programs are too small and erratic to have had much impact.

Pastoral development is a complicated issue. On the one hand, pastoralists understand livestock production in arid lands range conservation, as well as traditional means of re-solving conflict and mediating disputes. However, prob-lems of increasing population growth and competition for pastures with farms, ranches, game parks, and towns which demands new solutions and innovative thinking about pastoralism. This can only be done by combining both indigenous and modern knowledge to solve the problems of human occupation of Africa's arid lands.

Development projects in Africa's pastoral regions have tended to follow one of three distinct approaches.

The Promotion of Commercial Livestock Production

This is the stated goal of most multilateral (World Bank) and bilateral (e.g., USAID) donor organizations, who seek to build a country's export earning power. Development projects in arid lands often encourage the creation of private ranches as superior to communal grazing regimes. Like the American West in the nineteenth century, commercial livestock ranches fence in the range, grow and sell predominantly young male animals, and exclude tribal and subsistence herders from markets and better grazing and water resources. Internationally assisted ranches have been developed in Botswana, Swaziland, South Africa, Zambia, Niger, Nigeria, Tanzania, and Kenya, with the model being Botswana, one of the few African countries with sufficient veterinary controls to export meat to the European Community. The process of commoditization divides up formerly communal shared grazing resources, and polarizes pastoral society into private ranchers and poor pastoralists.

The Provision of Massive Food Aid and Famine Relief to Pastoralist Communities

These efforts often continue long after a drought crisis has passed, and contributes to the creation of large dependent populations as among the Turkana described in Chapter 2. Oxfam International, a major relief organization, has criticized long-term famine-relief projects as an inappropriate and destructive form of development assistance, since donated grains intended as food supplements quickly become the primary food source for settled populations, replacing local food production and ultimately leading to greater malnutrition.

Alternative and Appropriate Development

The least funded, but potentially the most successful of development approaches, aims to support traditional pastoral economies with improvements in animal husbandry, veterinary care, and range conservation. Oxfam, for example, has joined other NGOs in concentrating on assisting pastoralists to feed themselves by providing low-cost technical assistance (e.g., veterinary medicines), improving traditional food production techniques (including restocking animals to impoverished pastoralists), conserving fuel wood through sales of fuel-efficient cookstoves, and searching for alternatives to traditional foods.

Why don't the major donors—the World Bank or USAID, for example—follow the lead of these smaller NGOs, whose activities are greeted with much more enthusiasm by rural populations (although not by urban bureaucrats) than the big multilateral projects? This is fundamentally a political and economic question, as the large international projects invariably start from the needs of the donor country rather than that of the aid recipients. Without sounding too cynical, the World Bank and USAID represent western economic interests who are mainly concerned with increasing export revenues from less developed countries to repay loans, and to encourage the donor countries to export expensive foreign technology and personnel. They favor policies promoting agricultural and mineral exports from the rural areas to the cities and from the less developed countries to the developed world.

SOME SUGGESTIONS

Development planners and government agencies need to appreciate that pastoral production systems are the result of generations of adaptive behavior and knowledge by populations in arid lands. Developers must observe how the traditional livestock economy is practiced and formulate policies for technical and economic assistance through consultation with the pastoralists themselves. After all, it is the camel, cattle, and small stock pastoralists themselves who are the true experts of food production in arid regions.

Pastoralists are not "anti-development." To the contrary, Ariaal are very vocal about what they want and need to improve their food security and stability. These demands include low-cost medicines and training in veterinary care; the building of water catchments to trap and hold rainfall (rather than mechanization of wells that only bring too many cattle to the water holes); and rational grazing controls that allow the pastoralist to graze their animals in normally restricted areas (e.g., forests) during emergency conditions. The solution to overgrazing is to enable pastoral herds to disperse over wide areas and away from urban centers. This can be achieved by a rational policy of water development and the provision of public security guaranteeing safety from theft. Mobility of the herding and livestock populations should be encouraged rather than discouraged. This can only be achieved by recognizing common property rights, the rights of independent peoples to their customary lands.

Market infrastructure should be improved by making stock routes, auctions, and competitive marketing available to the pastoralist. Cooperatives for transporting and selling livestock should be encouraged, with profits used to hire drivers, veterinary officers, and security. Extension services in education, business and accounting skills, and livestock management should be increased.

Urban migration, sedentarization, wage labor and agriculture are facts on the ground for pastoralists today. New job opportunities related to the economic growth of pastoral populations should be encouraged with appropriate training programs offered in construction, health services, and transportation. It is particularly important to train local health, veterinary, and marketing officers recruited directly from the pastoralists themselves.

Institutions empowering the rural pastoralists need to be strengthened, both in political and economic arenas. This includes democratically elected representatives from the local settlement, town councils, county council, and parliamentary seats, a policy that is presently in effect in Kenya. But more than token political office, pastoralists need to control their own resources. In particular, herding cooperatives with marketing quotas and fair prices and banking institutions rewarding savings and offering low-cost credits would enable the pastoralists to have some security against the vagaries of environmental stress and economic hardship. These ideas are currently being discussed and promoted not only by NGOs but by the World Bank and other large funders.

Finally, efforts to promote conservation need to be supported and expanded. Tree planting is a positive example of a conservation effort that is having a visible effect in the towns of Korr, Ngurunit, and Karare, offering shade, protection against wind, and, most importantly, firewood, the region's only fuel. The development of low-cost electrical power by wind generators is already occurring in the arid regions of Africa including Marsabit Town, and shows great potential for the future.

The Ariaal are growing as a successful community of herders and now farmers. If the they can retain control of their grazing and farming resources, and if development efforts focus on the suggestions raised above, the Ariaal will continue to remain a vibrant, and to me, fascinating community.

Recommended Reading

CHAPTER 1. ARIAAL: STUDYING AN EAST AFRICAN PASTORALIST SOCIETY

Barfield, Thomas J.
  1993.   *The Nomadic Alternative.* Englewood Cliffs, N.J.:
            Prentice Hall.

Fratkin, Elliot.
  1986.   Stability and Resilience in East African Pastoralism:
            The Ariaal and Rendille of Northern Kenya. *Human
            Ecology* 14 (3):269–286.

  1989.   Household Variation and Gender Inequality in
            Ariaal Pastoral Production: Results of a Stratified
            Time Allocation Survey. *American Anthropologist* 91
            (2):45–55.

  1997.   Pastoralism: Governance and Development Issues.
            Annual Reviews in Anthropology, Volume 26.

Fratkin, Elliot, Kathleen Galvin, and Eric A. Roth (eds.).
  1994.   *African Pastoralist Systems: An Integrated Approach.*
            Boulder: Lynne Rienner Publishers.

Fratkin, Elliot, and Eric A. Roth.
  1990.   Drought and Economic Differentiation among Ariaal
            pastoralists of Kenya. *Human Ecology* 18 (4): 385–402.

Galaty, John G., and Pierre Bonte.
  1991.   *Herders, Warriors, and Traders: Pastoralism in Africa,*
            J. G. Galaty and P. Bonte (eds.), pp. 267–292. Boulder:
            Westview Press.

Galaty, John G., and Douglas L. Johnson.
1990.   *The World of Pastoralism.* New York, The Guilford Press.

Smith, Andrew.
1992.   *Pastoralism in Africa.* London: Hurst and Co.

Spencer, Paul.
1998.   *The Pastoral Continuum: The Marginalization of Tradi-
             tion in East Africa.* Oxford: Oxford University Press.

CHAPTER 2. DROUGHT, DEVELOPMENT, AND KENYA'S PASTORALISTS

Berman, Bruce, and John Lonsdale.
1992.   *Unhappy Valley: Conflict in Kenya and Africa. Book One:
             State and Class.* James Curry, London.

Campbell, David J.
1993.   Land as Ours, Land as Mine: Economic, Political and
             Ecological Marginalization in Kajiado District. In *Be-
             ing Maasai*, T. Spear and R. Waller (eds.), pp. 258–272.
             London: James Curry Publishers.

Dyson-Hudson, Rada, and J. Terrence McCabe.
1985.   *South Turkana Nomadism: Coping with an Unpredictably
             Varying Environment.* Human Relations Area Files
             Ethnography series FL 17-001. New Haven: HRAF.

Galaty, John G.
1993.   Maasai Expansion and the New East African Pasto-
             ralism. In *Being Maasai*, T. Spear and R. Waller (eds.),
             pp. 61–86. London: James Curry Publishers.

1994.   Rangeland Tenure and Pastoralism in Africa. In
             African Pastoralist Systems, E. Fratkin, K. Galvin,
             and E. A. Roth (eds.), pp. 185–204. Boulder: Lynne
             Rienner Publishers.

Hodgson, Dorothy.
2001   *Once Intrepid Warriors: Gender, Ethnicity, and the Cul-
             tural Politics of Maasai Development.* Bloomington: In-
             diana University Press.

Hogg, Richard.
1982.   Destitution and Development: The Turkana of
             Northwest Kenya. *Disasters* 6 (3):164–168.

Homewood, Kathleen, and William A. Rodgers.
1991.   *Maasailand Ecology.* Cambridge: Cambridge University Press.

Lamphear, John.
1992.   *The Scattering Time: Turkana Responses to Colonial Rule.* Oxford: Clarendon Press.

Little, P. D.
1992.   *The Elusive Granary.* Cambridge: Cambridge University Press.

McCabe, J. Terrence.
1990.   Turkana Pastoralism: A Case against the Tragedy of the Commons. *Human Ecology* 18:81–104.

Saitoti, Tepilit Ole.
1988.   The worlds of a Maasai warrior: an autobiography. Berkeley: University of California Press.

Schlee, Günther.
1989.   *Identities on the Move.* Manchester University Press.

Sobania, Neal W.
1988.   Pastoralist Migration and Colonial Policy: A Case Study from Northern Kenya. In *The Ecology of Survival: Case Studies from North East African History,* D. Johnson and D. Anderson (eds.) pp. 219–239. London: Crook Greene.

Spear, Thomas, and Richard Waller.
1993.   *Being Maasai: Ethnicity and Identity in East Africa.* London: James Currey.

Talle, Aud.
1988.   *Women at a Loss: Changes in Maasai Pastoralism and their effects on Gender Relations.* Stockholm Studies in Social Anthropology, 19. Stockholm: Department of Social Anthropology, University of Stockholm.

Waller, Richard.
1988.   Emutai: Crisis and Response in Maasailand 1883–1902. In D. Johnson and D. Anderson (eds.) *The Ecology of Survival,* pp. 73–112. London: Lester Crook Academic Publishing.

CHAPTER 3. ARIAAL IDENTITY AND CULTURE

Fratkin, Elliot.
1991.   *Surviving Drought and Development*. Boulder: Westview Press.

1991.   The Laibon as Sorcerer: A Samburu Laibon among the Ariaal, 1973:1987. *Africa* 61 (3):318–333.

1996.   Traditional Medicine and Concepts of Healing among Samburu Pastoralists of Kenya. *Journal of Ethnobiology* 16 (1):63–100.

Hodgson, Dorothy.
2000.   *Rethinking Pastoralism in Africa: Gender, Culture and the Myth of the Patriarchal Pastoralist*. Oxford: James Currey; Athens OH: Ohio University Press.

Llewellyn-Davies, Melissa.
1981.   Women, warriors, and patriarchs. In *Sexual Meanings*, S. Ortner and J. Whitehead (eds.), pp. 330–58. Cambridge: Cambridge University Press.

Shell-Duncan, Bettina, and Ylva Hernlund.
2000.   *Female 'Circumcision' In Africa: Culture, Controversy and Change*. Boulder: Lynne Rienner Publishers.

Spencer, Paul.
1965.   *The Samburu: A Study of Gerontocracy in a Nomadic Tribe*. Berkeley: University of California Press.

1973.   *Nomads in Alliance*. London: Oxford University Press.

CHAPTER 4. A PASTORAL LIFE: LIVESTOCK PRODUCTION AND HUMAN NUTRITION

Dahl, Gudrun, and Anders Hjort.
1976.   *Having Herds: Pastoral Herd Growth and Household Economy*. Stockholm Studies in Social Anthropology 2. Stockholm: Dept. of Social Anthropology, University of Stockholm.

Dyson-Hudson, Neville, and Rada Dyson-Hudson.
1982.   The Structure of East African herds and the Future of East African Herders. *Development and Change* 13: 213–238.

Galvin, Kaltheen, D. Layne Coppock, and Paul W. Leslie.
1994.   Diet, Nutrition, and the Pastoral Strategy. In *African Pastoralist Systems*, E. Fratkin, K. Galvin, and E. A. Roth (eds.), pp. 113–132. Boulder: Lynne Rienner Publishers.

IPAL.
1984.   *Integrated Resource Assessment and Management Plan for Western Marsabit District, Northern Kenya.* Integrated Project in Arid Lands Technical Report No. A-6. Nairobi: UNESCO.

Little, M. A., and P. W. Leslie (eds.).
1999.   *Turkana Herders of the Dry Savanna: Ecology and Biobehavioral Response of Nomads to an Uncertain Environment.* New York: Oxford University Press.

Sato, Shun.
1980.   Pastoral movements and the subsistence unit of the Rendille of northern Kenya. Africa 2:1–78. Senri Ethnological Studies 6. Osaka: National Museum of Ethnology.

Schwartz, H. Jürgen, and M. Dioli.
1992.   *The One-Humped Camel (Camelus dromedarius) in Eastern Africa.* Weikersheim, Germany: Verlag Josef Margraf.

Schwartz, H. Jürgen, S. Shaabani, and D. Walther.
1991.   *Range Management Handbook of Kenya,* Volume II: Marsabit District. Nairobi: Republic of Kenya, Ministry of Livestock Development.

CHAPTER 6. FARMS, TOWNS, AND THE FUTURE OF THE ARIAAL

Baxter, Paul.
1991.   *When The Grass is Gone: Development Intervention in African Arid Lands.* Scandinavian Institute of African Studies, Uppsala.

Dyson-Hudson, Neville.
1991.   Pastoral production systems and livestock development projects: An East African perspective. In *Putting People First: Sociological Variables in Rural Development,* ed. Michael M. Cernea, 2nd edition, 219–256. New York: The World Bank, Oxford University Press.

Fratkin, Elliot, and Kevin Smith.
1995.   Women's Changing Economic Roles with Pastoral Sedentarization: Varying Strategies in Four Rendille Communities. *Human Ecology* 23 (4):433–454.

Fratkin, Elliot, Martha A. Nathan, and Eric A. Roth.
1999.   "Health Consequences of Pastoral Sedentarization Among Rendille of Northern Kenya." In David M. Anderson and Vigdis Broch-Due (eds.) *The Poor are*

Not Us: Poverty and Pastoralism, pp. 149–163. Oxford: James Currey Ltd.

Hill, Allen G.
1985.   *Population, Health and Nutrition in the Sahel.* London: Routledge and Kegan Paul.

Little, P. D.
1994   "The Social Context of Land Degradation ("Deserti-fication") in Dry Regions." In *Population and Environment: Rethinking the Debate*, L. Arizpe, M. P. Stone, and D. C. Major (eds.), pp. 209–251. Boulder: West-view Press.

Nathan, Martha A., Elliot Fratkin, and Eric A. Roth.
1996.   Sedentism and Child Health among Rendille Pasto-ralists of Northern Kenya. *Social Science and Medicine* 43 (4):503–515.

O'Leary, Michael F.
1990.   Drought and Change Amongst Northern Kenya No-madic Pastoralists: The Case of the Rendille and Gabra. In *From Water to World Making: African Models and Arid Lands*, Gisli Palsson (ed.), pp. 151–174. Upp-sala: Scandinavian Institute of African Studies.

Roth, Eric A.
1991.   Education, tradition, and household labor among Rendille pastoralists of N. Kenya. *Human Organization* 50:136–141.

Salih, Mohamed A. Mohamed.
1991.   Livestock Development or Pastoral Development? In *When the Grass is gone: Development intervention in African Arid Lands*, P. T. W. Baxter, ed. Pp. 37–57. Upp-sala: The Scandinavian Institute of African Studies.

Wario, Adano Roba, and Karen Witsenburg.
(In Press).   Once Nomads Settle: Assessing the Process on Mars-abit Mountain. In Elliot Fratkin and Eric A. Roth *As Pastoralists Settle: Social, Economic, and Health Conse-quences of Pastoral Sedentarization among Rendille of Northern Kenya*. Bergin and Garvey Publishers.